The War of Independence

A Declaration

MAURICE SAATCHI & PETER WARBURTON

An approach to the No 1 problem of the 21st Century: taxes are always going up, yet the government never seems to have enough money to spend on good things like health and education

CENTRE FOR POLICY STUDIES
57 Tufton Street, London SW1P 3QL
1999

THE AUTHORS

Maurice Saatchi graduated from the London School of Economics and Political Science in 1967 with First Class Honours in Economics. He won the MacMillan Prize for Sociology in that year. He was the co-founder of Saatchi & Saatchi Advertising and is now a partner in M & C Saatchi. He is a Governor of the London School of Economics and a Member of the Council of the Royal College of Art. He was elevated to the peerage in 1996.

Dr Peter Warburton is economic adviser to Robert Fleming, an international investment banking group. He previously worked as an economic researcher, forecaster and lecturer at the London Business School and the City University. He is a member of the Shadow Monetary Policy Committee at the Institute of Economic Affairs and has recently published his first book, *Debt and Delusion* (Allen Lane, 1999).

Acknowledgements

The authors wish to thank Jeremy Sinclair and Steve Hilton, without whom this pamphlet would not exist. Support for this publication was given by the Institute for Policy Research.

ISBN No. 1 897969 91 0

Printed by the Chameleon Press, 5 – 25 Burr Road, London SW18

CONTENTS

SUMMARY

- Britain's system of tax and spending is 200 years old this year; it needs modernisation.

- The present system causes a 'double whammy' – taxes always go up, but there is always a shortage of money for good things like health and education.

- The overall tax burden has risen from below 30% of UK GDP in the 1950s, to 37% in 1998, defeating many determined efforts to reduce it.

- International comparisons suggest that a higher tax burden is associated with weaker economic performance – and less money to spend on public services in the long run.

- It is time to declare a War of Independence, a War which aims to return taxation to 1950s levels, and, at the same time, to provide more funds for health and education.

- 'Independence Day' – the day on which people stop working for the government and start working for themselves – should be moved back from 18 May where it is today to 21 April, where it was in the 1950s.

- 'Independence Day' should be declared a national holiday, a benchmark of progress towards the goal of greater independence for all.

THE WAR OF INDEPENDENCE – A DECLARATION

- As a first step, three proposals are put forward for consideration:

1 End the overlap between taxes and benefits

First, the massive overlap between tax and benefit payments needs examination. Under the present system, the government collects between £30 billion and £40 billion in Income Tax and National Insurance contributions from around 17 million households with incomes below £20,000 a year, of whom 7 million earn less than £10,000 a year. Yet the government also distributes £30 billion to £40 billion in benefits (see Appendix 1) to the same people. Cancellation of this overlap achieves more than half the aims of the War of Independence, reducing the tax burden from 37% to 33% of national income.

The objective is to establish 'crossover points' for each household type, below which people receive benefit payments *from* the government, and above which they make tax payments *to* the government. In the great majority of cases, individuals would then be either benefit recipients, or taxpayers, but not both at the same time.

2 Exchange allowances for lower tax rates

There are over 250 tax allowances, reliefs and exemptions (see Appendix 2) which taxpayers can claim. Not surprisingly, this complex web has created a wide disparity between the gross and the net tax system. Currently, the government can raise in tax 53% of national income (£434 billion) but a third of this, £134 billion (16% of GDP), can be claimed back by companies and individuals through tax allowances and reliefs. This leaves the government with net proceeds of around £300 billion. This mass of complex allowances, preferences, credits, tax breaks, indexations and marginal adjustments should be exchanged for a more open, transparent system of lower tax rates. This would have the additional benefit of reducing governments' scope for 'hidden' tax increases.

3 Merge government departments

Following the above two modernisations, the Inland Revenue, the Department of Social Security, the Benefits Agency, and the Contributions Agency would be merged. This merger would result in a 20% to 30% saving in administration costs, through the elimination of duplicated tax and benefit assessments, and a more efficient benefit payments system. All of this £5 billion saving could be used to boost investment in health and education.

- The results of such a new system could be that nearly 12 million people stop paying Income Tax: about 8.6 million working people with annual incomes below £15,000, and most of the 3.4 million taxpayers aged 65 and over.

- A research programme is needed to assess the feasibility of this reform and to investigate the options for its implementation. When a simplified, streamlined structure is established, it would cut the tax burden, improve Britain's long-term economic performance, and provide more funds for health and education.

It is time to declare war. A War of Independence. Its aim is to focus public attention on the benefits of bringing forward Britain's Independence Day from 18 May to 21 April.

CHAPTER ONE

INTRODUCTION

AS WELL AS BEING ON THE edge of a new Millennium, 1999 is the bicentenary of the introduction of Income Tax into Britain. What better time for a radical look at the tax and spending system that has developed over those 200 years.

How tedious, the reader might say. Haven't there been endless such papers over the years? Learned works. Erudite pamphlets. Detailed exercises in economic modelling. What is the point of another one?

There have indeed been thousands of papers written about our system of tax and spending. Nevertheless, this paper is meant to be different. While the parameters of our tax and spending system are the bricks and mortar of the building, that is not what this paper is *about*. This paper is about the architecture.

We have all become painfully familiar with the structure of our tax and spending; taxes always seem to go up, yet governments never seem to have enough money to spend on health, education and the public services.

This paper is about independence. Why independence is a good thing. How much of it we have lost. How we could get some of it back.

The possibility of a radical reform is raised in the hope that it may stimulate debate. With such a reform, the government would be able to meet the legitimate requirements of its citizens without undermining their independence by ever-higher taxes.

The UK Tax Burden

This paper is about independence. Why independence is a good thing. How much of it we have lost. How we could get some of it back.

FIGURE 1.1 UK Tax Burden in the Last 40 Years

Year	Total Taxation & NICs £ millions	Nominal GDP £ millions	Tax Burden %
1948	4,170	11,835	35.2
	4,474	12,565	35.6
1950	4,501	13,112	34.3
	4,836	14,612	33.1
1952	5,094	15,764	32.3
	5,164	16,906	30.5
1954	5,355	17,890	29.9
	5,735	19,304	29.7
1956	5,983	20,766	28.8
	6,373	21,920	29.1
1958	6,786	22,853	29.7
	7,044	24,213	29.1
1960	7,242	25,887	28.0
	8,024	27,432	29.3
1962	8,784	28,812	30.5
	9,008	30,856	29.2
1964	9,762	33,435	29.2
	10,996	36,035	30.5
1966	12,086	38,370	31.5
	13,500	40,400	33.4
1968	15,226	43,808	34.8
	17,105	47,153	36.3
1970	19,220	52,370	36.7
	20,461	58,294	35.1
1972	21,826	66,747	32.7
	25,011	74,661	33.5
1974	32,214	89,733	35.9
	40,374	111,222	36.3
1976	46,606	130,185	35.8
	52,470	151,648	34.6
1978	59,018	174,610	33.8
	73,150	209,598	34.9
1980	85,870	237,209	36.2
	101,270	259,667	39.0
1982	109,467	284,330	38.5
	117,843	308,489	38.2
1984	127,440	331,875	38.4
	138,333	364,035	38.0
1986	148,516	394,989	37.6
	162,135	434,679	37.3
1988	177,616	482,653	36.8
	192,675	525,000	36.7
1990	205,548	566,247	36.3
	205,297	578,302	35.5
1992	205,935	609,276	33.8
	214,889	643,379	33.4
1994	234,524	681,755	34.4
	254,996	720,327	35.4
1996	269,262	760,628	35.4
	293,958	807,576	36.4
1998	318,060	855,000	37.2

Sources: Inland Revenue Statistics and the Pre-Budget Report, November 1998

INTRODUCTION

The aim of the War of Independence is to bring about an outcome which is – superficially at least – a modest and unexceptional one. The specific objective is to turn back the clock to the early 1950s, in terms of the UK's overall tax burden, and yet achieve higher spending on health and education.

Between 1955 and 1964, the total UK tax burden averaged 29.3% of the money value of Gross Domestic Product, with little variation from year to year. As figure 1.1 shows, this was no flash in the pan; it was achieved over a 10-year period, equivalent to two complete business cycles.

At that time, the government's current income from taxation was more than sufficient to cover its current expenditure on goods and services, social security, pensions and benefits.

For a variety of reasons, Harold Wilson's Labour Governments of 1964-70 intervened heavily in the economy, raising tax revenues to match the substantial increases in public spending. By 1970, the tax take had risen to almost 37% of GDP.

Since then, five Conservative Governments have worked hard to undo this expansion of public sector influence. But the sustained efforts of the Thatcher and Major administrations did not succeed. In fact, the overall tax burden in 1998 was again over 37% of GDP. By 2002, Labour's plans are expected to carry the total tax take above 39%, which would represent a peacetime record. Despite this remorseless increase in taxation, it is unlikely that the government's current income will match its current expenditure even then.

European developments make the task more urgent

As far as tax and spending are concerned, Britain may be on the wrong path. But other European countries are further down that path than we are. Economic and Monetary Union, to which process Britain is a full signatory, will inevitably lead to pressure for Britain to fall into line with continental European approaches to tax and spending; to travel even more quickly down the wrong path. We have already seen the initial skirmishes in this battle, which the Government, admirably enough, has stated that it will fight with vigour on our behalf. The importance of victory in this battle can immediately be seen from a glance at the tax and spending position in other EU member states. In 1995, when Britain's tax burden was still 35.3%, the EU average was 41.8%, with Germany at 39.2%, France at 44.5% and Denmark at 51.3%. If such high levels of taxation are required in peacetime, what would happen if Britain or Europe ever embarked on a prolonged war?

The more the UK government looks for its direction and its policies to the continent of Europe, the greater will be the pressure for the UK tax burden to rise. This would lead automatically to a further loss of individual independence in Britain.

FIGURE 1.2 Comparative Taxation Trends in the EU and the UK

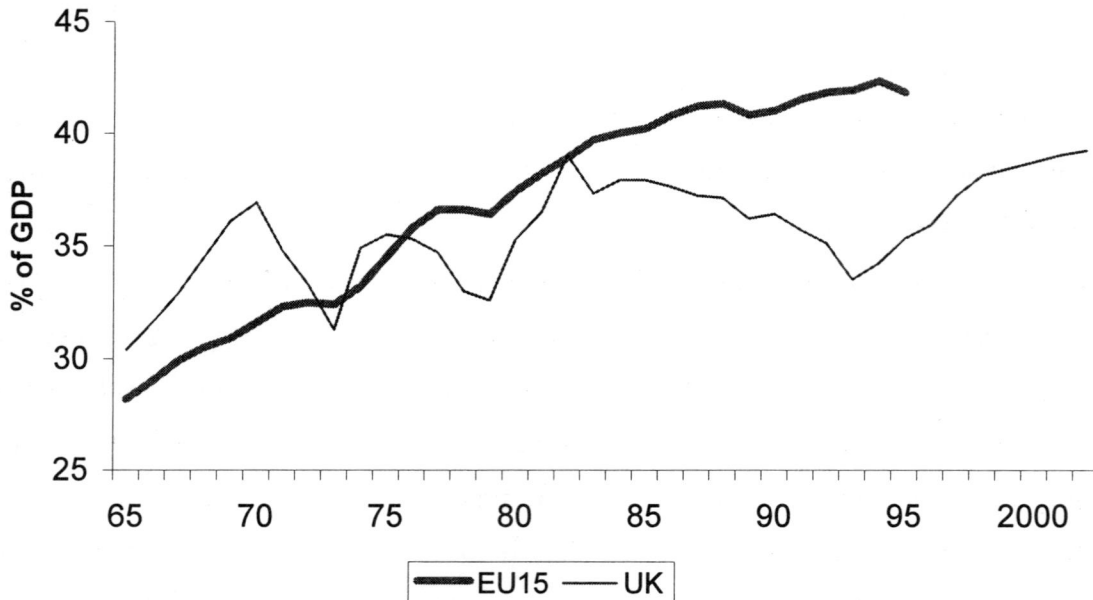

Sources: OECD Revenue Statistics, 1997 edition and Financial Statement and Budget Report, March 1998

The path we are on leads to moral problems too

Quite apart from its severe economic effects, our system of tax and spending creates damaging moral and social conditions. The principle that links taxation to morality is not new. King Edward I expressed it simply:

> *To each his own! We must find out what is ours, and due to us.*
> *And others, what is theirs, and due to them.*

It is easy to forget the basic function of tax. Its purpose is to pay for things that individuals cannot reasonably or efficiently provide for themselves: defence, education, police, hospitals. But currently its effect is to deny people the most basic of human rights – the right to work and the freedom to determine their own spending priorities. Whether intentional or not, it is immoral to lead the country down a path to poverty and unemployment.

INTRODUCTION

The pursuit of fairness in taxation has created much that is unfair. In any case, fairness is nothing without independence – which should be the ultimate aim. All proposals for reform should work to this end. Independence is a fine and noble objective for any political party, for only independence can guarantee social justice through personal dignity.

Independence is a fine and noble objective for any political party.

Yet more and more people in Britain are becoming dependent on the state. The phrase 'dependency culture' has now become firmly established in the lexicon of political life. The dependency culture itself has become ever more firmly entrenched in our national life. How do we hope to ensure a national future of decency and fairness, where every citizen grows up knowing they have the means and the opportunity to make something of their lives, when in Britain, proportionately more children than anywhere else in the world are born into a family that is primarily dependent on the state for its purchasing power? What is moral about national strategies for turning the 'have-nots' into 'haves' when the very policies serve only to reinforce the conditions and divisions that turned them into 'have-nots' in the first place?

A new approach
The basic arguments in favour of less tax, more independence and more individual choice have, in recent years, achieved almost universal victories in the battle of ideas. Both major political parties in Britain have made some attempts to follow this agenda. Peter Lilley's reforms of social security, and now Alastair Darling's own initiatives, demonstrate the political consensus that has been achieved. However, is it enough just to change politicians? Or does Britain need to change path?

Attempts at tinkering with the tax and benefit system, rather than redesigning it, have failed. Incremental and piecemeal reform has been the enemy of the best intentions, on all sides. While small steps have been taken in the right direction, the fundamental issues have not been addressed. To break free, the system must be redesigned in the interests of promoting economic growth and employment prospects over a much longer horizon. Rather than focusing on the incremental effects of this or that minor change, the objective should be to create an environment in which people are prepared to accept radical change. So the War of Independence is less about theoretical battles than about their translation into radical, but practical, policy reforms.

This paper sets out the practical principles on which the War of Independence can be fought – principles which are relatively uncontroversial. It also puts forward some real-world proposals – proposals which will be extremely controversial. These proposals are put forward in the certainty that even those who may secretly agree with them in theory will find thoroughly worthy public objections to their practical implementation. Those pantomime dames of Her Majesty's Treasury are expected to make an appearance on stage: 'transitional problems'; 'winners and losers'; 'revenue shortfalls.' Their dubious charms should be rejected and a more attractive prospect considered: the chance to revitalise and restructure the current system of tax and spending as we enter a new millennium, for the benefit of all.

> A more attractive prospect should be considered: the chance to revitalise and restructure the current system of tax and spending as we enter a new millennium, for the benefit of all.

How the reader might react

If our country is to be more successful, its people more prosperous, and our lives more independent, we can no longer accept the continuing growth of government expenditure and its corollary: the encroachment on our independence. So it is necessary to create a climate in which radical and controversial action in the field of tax and spending is not something to be worried about, but something to be enthusiastic about. Then our political leaders will be able to act.

So if there were to be one reaction to these proposals, the one which would give the greatest satisfaction, it would be a simple one: *'Why not?'*

CHAPTER TWO

THE WAR OF INDEPENDENCE: A SIMPLE OBJECTIVE

A SIMPLE QUESTION HAS TROUBLED British governments for years: how to spend more money on good things like health and education without taking away people's independence with ever-increasing taxes? While this paper outlines one answer (otherwise there would be no point in publishing the paper at all), it makes no claim to have *all* the answers.

Many serious attempts have been made to address this issue in the past. But consider the arguments on their merit. If they are found convincing, then more research will be required to examine in detail their practical implementation.

An uncontroversial observation: we are on the wrong path

Our present system of tax and spending is not something that has changed significantly from day to day, year to year, government to government. It is the result of the practices that we have followed, and the institutions that we have developed. We are where we are because of the path we have followed.

Consider the path that we are on. Sooner or later the British economy will move into recession. For governments, whatever their political composition, recessions lead to budget pressures: government receipts tend to fall, and demands on the public purse tend to rise. Admirably enough, the current British Government has stated that it will not allow our public finances to deteriorate, whatever economic circumstances may bring. There will be no irresponsible borrowing.

So what is to be done? In an economic slowdown, if the budget is to remain broadly in balance, either tax burdens must go up or spending must come down. Judging from the plans set out in its Red Book, the New Labour Government has decided to raise tax. Just like the last Conservative Government.

These habitual responses to economic difficulty illustrate the main problems identified in this paper. Faced with the legitimate need to maintain sound public finances, successive British governments, both Labour and Conservative, have chosen to raise the overall burden of taxation. This has been going on for over 40 years.

As a result, the government spends almost 40% of national income (see figure 2.1). To put it another way, close to half of the spending decisions that are taken in Britain are not taken by individuals, but by the government, on their behalf. But apart from a small amount of capital income and rent, the government has no money of its own: all the remaining spending has to be paid for by the people.

FIGURE 2.1 The Structure of Government Expenditure

	£ billion	Share (%)
Social Security and Housing Benefits *of which:*	105.2	32.9
- National Insurance benefits and pensions	44.8	14.0
- Social assistance benefits in cash	60.4	18.9
Education	36.2	11.3
Health	35.3	11.0
Defence	20.9	6.5
Other Local Government (England)	14.8	4.6
Home Office, Cabinet Office and legal departments	13.3	4.2
Scotland	12.9	4.0
Environment and transport	9.7	3.0
Wales	6.5	2.0
Northern Ireland	5.5	1.7
Trade and Industry, Culture, Media and Sport	4.9	1.5
Agriculture, Fisheries and Food & CAP	4.1	1.3
FCO and International Development	3.3	1.0
Social Security (administration)	3.3	1.0
Net payments to EC institutions	2.1	0.7
Central Government gross debt interest	28.3	8.8
Accounting and other adjustments	13.5	4.2
Total Managed Expenditure	**319.8**	**100.0**
GDP at current market prices	813.6	
TME as a % of GDP	**39.3**	

Source: ONS Financial Statistics, October 1998

So today, government has to take away around 37% of earnings through a complex range of taxes (see figure 2.2). In other words, for almost five months of the year, British people are working to pay for the government. Whether it is Income Tax, VAT, Corporation Tax, or any other form of tax, the people pay. Of course, the government does not just keep this money. It gives it back to people through social security benefits, the provision of national defence, the NHS, the education system and so on. One can

> **Most British governments since the Second World War have been elected on a promise to keep taxes down. Yet most left office with taxes higher than when they came to power.**

argue endlessly about the rights and wrongs of these expenditures. But what is unarguable is that for every pound spent *by* the government, individuals are dependent *on* the government for that particular item of expenditure. By taking away our money, and then deciding how to spend it, the government is taking away our independence. And over the last 40 years, more and more of it has been forfeited.

FIGURE 2.2: How we are taxed

	£ billion	£ billion	Share (%)
Personal taxation			
Income tax and capital gains tax	81.8		27.3
Council tax and motor vehicle duty	14.0		4.7
National Insurance contributions	21.5		7.2
Value added tax	55.6		18.5
Other taxes and duties on products	44.8		14.9
Inheritance tax	1.7		0.6
Total personal taxation		**219.4**	**73.1**
Taxes levied on companies:			
Corporation tax	30.4		
Employers' National Insurance contributions	29.6		
Non-domestic rates	14.9		
PRT, windfall utilities tax and other business taxes	5.7		
Total taxes levied on companies		**80.6**	**26.9**
Total personal and company taxation		**300.0**	**100.0**
GDP at current market prices		813.6	
Total taxes as a % of GDP		**36.9**	

Source: ONS Financial Statistics, October 1998

THE WAR OF INDEPENDENCE – A DECLARATION

Most British governments since the Second World War have been elected on a promise to keep taxes down. Yet most left office with taxes higher than when they came to power. The tax burden has gone up, whichever party has been in government. So for 40 years our independence has been eroded. And some extraordinary anomalies have been created.

First, the absurdity of overlapping payments

Bizarrely, Britain's tax and benefit system today needlessly transfers between £30 and £40 billion a year (9% to 12% of all government spending) in and out of the very same households, because of the overlap between taxpayers and recipients of state-administered benefits and pensions. Last year, the number of individual Income Tax payers rose to 26.1 million (more than ever before). Tens of millions of benefit claims are paid each week, many of which are income top-ups and housing subsidies to tax-paying working households. How much better it would be if these households simply

> ## Britain's tax and benefit system today needlessly transfers between £30 and £40 billion a year in and out of the very same households.

retained a larger proportion of their earned income. Higher net incomes decrease the need for government benefit payments. The requirement for millions of minor tax and benefit transfers would simply disappear. Without detracting from the overall generosity of the welfare system, the cancellation of overlapping payments would set the UK on a different path.

The extensive and complex system of tax and spending has brought many material advantages to the people of Britain. But it has also produced some strange results. Remember that the government spends almost 40% of national income. Bear in mind also that roughly a third of this spending goes on social security benefits of one kind or another. Then consider:

- The national average income for a man in full-time employment is £21,600 a year.
- Yet 4.4 million people who have total incomes of under £5,000 a year still pay tax.
- Another 3.6 million taxpayers have total incomes of between £5,000 and £7,500 a year.
- Another 6.2 million taxpayers have total incomes of between £7,500 and £10,000 a year.
- At the same time, the great majority of these 14.2 million people – all of whom pay tax to the government – also receive means-tested benefits from the government.

And second, the absurdity of mass 'allowances'

The UK, in common with many other countries, has an extensive array of tax exemptions, special allowances and reliefs (see Appendix I). Some are designed to promote pensions, savings and investment; some to shield expenditures on food and clothing; some to make home ownership more affordable and others to favour small businesses. However, the more complicated the structure of taxation, the greater are its likely adverse side effects. In addition, the greater the value of allowances and other concessions, the larger the gross (or notional) tax system that is required to raise a particular amount of net revenue. Figure 2.3 provides some approximate calculations of the size of the gross tax structure as it stood in the 1997-98 fiscal year. If it were unrelieved by allowances and exemptions, the present structure would be capable of collecting tax revenues equivalent to around 53% of national income. Through the gradual erosion of allowances, a UK government could achieve EU average levels of taxation almost imperceptibly.

FIGURE 2.3 Structure of the UK taxation system (1997-98)

	Tax paid £ billion	Estimated value of tax reliefs £ billion	Notional taxation £ billion
Income, capital gains tax and IHT	83.5	63.6	147.1
Council tax and motor vehicle duty	14.0	7.3	21.3
National Insurance contributions	21.5	10.3	31.8
VAT	55.6	28.5	84.1
Other taxes and duties on products	44.8	0.0	44.8
Taxes levied on companies	80.6	25.2	105.8
Totals	**300.0**	**134.9**	**434.9**
Total tax as a % of GDP at market prices	36.9	16.6	53.5
Principal tax reliefs:			
Personal income tax thresholds		29.6	
Zero-rated VAT items		20.6	
Occupational and personal pension relief		19.2	
Capital investment allowances (companies)		17.1	
Other income tax allowances		16.2	
Exemptions from VAT		8.0	
Other corporation tax and PRT reliefs		8.0	
Inheritance tax and stamp duty reliefs		7.3	
Capital gains tax relief		6.2	
Other National Insurance reliefs		2.7	
Total		**134.9**	

Sources: HM Treasury Tax Ready Reckoner and Reliefs, December 1997; ONS Financial Statistics Table S30, October 1998

In 1997-8 the unrelieved taxable potential of the present tax structure levied by the Exchequer on companies and individuals amounted to £434.9 billion. But an astonishing £134.9 billion, almost a third of the total, is given back in the form of reliefs and allowances.

THE WAR OF INDEPENDENCE – A DECLARATION

The charm of such a large gross tax system – from the government's point of view – is the scope it allows for hidden tax increases via reduced allowances. Under the present structure, a Chancellor of Exchequer can increase tax without ever announcing a 'tax rise'. Chancellors, being human, have not resisted this temptation, with the result that tax as a percentage of GDP creeps up invisibly, with little political impact. 'Invisible' tax increases, by definition, are not seen; and not being seen, are not felt. Appendix 3 shows

Oh what a tangled web!

how the recent Budget changes to income tax rates (the 10p starting rate and the 22p band) are dealt with in two lines, whereas another 62 lines are required to describe changes to allowances, reliefs and exemptions. Oh what a tangled web!

Under the proposals outlined in this paper, governments would be obliged to display greater transparency in their tax policies. Full disclosure would mean governments could not hide from the political consequences of their tax actions. By exchanging the mass of complex allowances for lower tax rates, the huge gulf between the gross and net tax system can be eliminated.

Governments would be obliged to display greater transparency in their tax policies, exchanging the mass of complex allowances for lower tax rates.

Successive administrations have made great virtue of cuts in the standard rate of Income Tax: the Chancellor, Gordon Brown, has introduced the new 10p tax band. Nevertheless, the personal Income Tax burden has increased due to the erosion of the real value of tax allowances, leaving a rising share of personal income liable to tax. Similarly, as UK VAT exemptions and zero-rated items become vulnerable to European tax harmonisation initiatives, the UK indirect tax burden could rise materially without any increase in the standard rate of VAT. One current EU proposal is to levy VAT in the country of origin rather than the country of destination. This would render the zero-rating of exports redundant and would threaten to remove zero-rating altogether in the UK.

An important consequence of the erosion of the real value of Income Tax allowances is that millions of lowly-paid and benefit-dependent individuals are also taxpayers. The extreme disincentives attaching to paid employment arise from the overlapping of low entry thresholds for tax and National Insurance contributions, with high marginal rates of withdrawal of social security benefits and privileges. The present system of housing benefits is a particular source of aggravation in this regard. The solutions presented in the March 1998 and 1999 Budgets (including the reform of National Insurance contributions, the Working Families Tax Credit and the forthcoming children's tax credit) point in the right direction but are too small to have a worthwhile impact.

Allowances help the better off

Another notable, if puzzling, feature of the development of the UK tax and benefits system is that the surge in the cost of transfer payments and the associated rise in the tax burden has been accompanied by widening income inequality in the adult population. According to a DSS study published in 1997, the lower half of the income distribution received 33% of total personal incomes in 1979 and 28% in 1994-95. The top 10% of the income distribution received 21% of the total in 1979 and 26% in 1994-95. Whatever purpose the increase in transfer payments was intended to achieve, it appears to have reinforced income inequality rather than the opposite.

Part of the explanation lies in that fact that wealthier individuals are able to structure their financial affairs so as to benefit from the vast array of exemptions and allowances. For example, in 1995 the £9.3 billion of tax relief for occupational pension contributions was distributed as follows: 2.3% for the poorest quintile of taxpayers; 5.3% for the second-lowest quintile; 9.5% for the middle quintile; 15.7% for the second-highest and 67.2% for the top quintile. Other examples of tax breaks that accrue disproportionately to the higher income groups are personal pension contributions, Tessas and Peps (now succeeded by Individual Savings Accounts), mortgage interest relief (soon to disappear), and expenditures, through trusts, on private education. Naturally, those with the largest potential tax liabilities make the greatest effort to discover legitimate ways of sheltering their income from taxation.

The tax structure promotes the hidden economy

The third undesirable feature of the present system is that it provides a significant incentive for sole proprietors and small businesses to operate outside the tax system. The size of the hidden, or black, economy in the UK has been estimated by Dr Bhattacharyya, of the University of Leicester, to have grown to between 7% and 10% of recorded GDP (equivalent to £57 billion and £80 billion for 1997-98). This implies a range for lost tax receipts of £20 billion to £28 billion, assuming a 35% average tax take on hidden earnings. Professor Kent Matthews, of Cardiff Business School, has identified a number of industries – such as restaurants, furniture and floorcoverings and hairdressing – in which actual VAT receipts fall well short of their predicted levels. The combination of a high VAT rate (17.5%) and a low registration threshold appears to have persuaded thousands of small businesses to operate outside the tax system. In a separate research study, Kent Matthews presents evidence to suggest that some EU countries have already raised their VAT rates to the point where the marginal tax take is actually declining, thereby reducing the public funds available for the health and education budgets.

In Britain today, there are proportionately more households with children without a wage-earner than in any other country in the developed world.

The path we're on has led us to some serious social problems

In Britain today, there are proportionately more households with children without a wage-earner than in any other country in the developed world: almost one household in five. Figure 2.4 shows how acute the problem has become. Yet, 20 years ago, fewer than one UK household in ten was workless.

FIGURE 2.4 Workless household rate by country for households with children, 1996 (%)

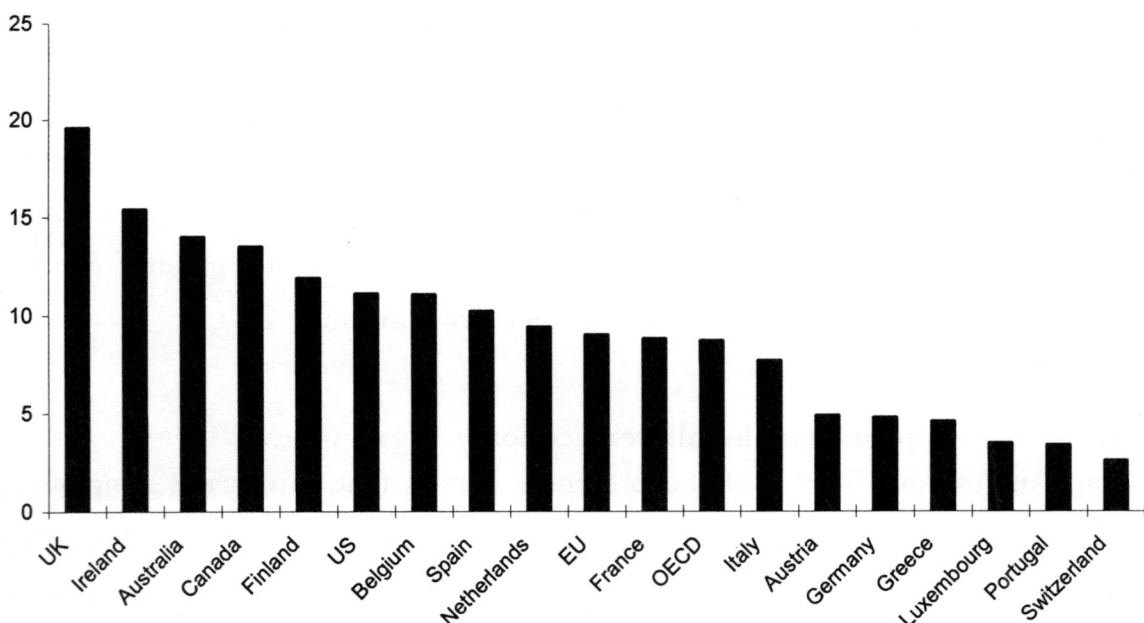

Source: Employment Policy Institute Employment Audit Issue 9, Autumn 1998

THE WAR OF INDEPENDENCE – A SIMPLE OBJECTIVE

This has brought about a remorseless increase, in communities all over Britain, of the linked problems which are now commonly described as 'social exclusion' – poor housing; poor public health; low standards of education, and high rates of crime. The tax and benefit system is supposed to make things better, through the redistribution of income and wealth. But instead, it is making things worse by reinforcing the very conditions that lead to social exclusion. At the same time, we are paying more tax than at any point in our peace-time history, which in itself inhibits the economic growth and job creation which could form part of the solution to the problems of social exclusion.

And, at the end of the day, the present system never seems to provide enough money for health and education, as we saw again in the latest NHS 'crisis' last winter.

What can be done?

This paper makes a plea for open-mindedness, a plea for tolerance. It is the obsession with the instant impact of any change to economic policy on any individual which has made British governments avoid decisions which would have ultimately benefited *every* individual.

We can measure our independence

The loss of individual independence is not a theoretical notion: it can be measured. Our independence can be gauged by measuring the proportion of our working year that is spent earning money that we pay to the government; by looking at the day on which we stop working for the government, and start working for ourselves and our families. That day is Independence Day. In 1999, it will fall on 18 May.

In many ways, it is outrageous that Independence Day falls so late in Britain today. We pride ourselves on being a 'free country.' Yet we tolerate a situation where the tax burden has reached near record proportions. It is as if we have all accepted as inevitable the combination of high taxation and inadequate public services.

It was not always like this

As little as 40 years ago, soon after the establishment of the modern welfare state, and before 'privatisation' was even thought of, the government accounted for just 30% of economic activity in Britain. In those days, Independence Day fell on 21 April, a full 27 days before it does today. The remorseless drift towards higher and higher taxes is not inevitable; there *is* a choice about which path to follow in the future. Moreover, if we continue on our present path, the consequences will be deeply damaging to social justice and economic efficiency in our country.

It need not be like this in the future

This paper proposes radical reform. Its aim is to create a society in which individuals are less dependent on the government for the ability to fulfil their potential. While the proposal is radical, its objective is relatively modest: to return us to the levels of tax and spending that we enjoyed in the 1950s.

In effect, this proposal is a declaration of war. The War of Independence. Its aim is to focus public attention on the benefits of bringing forward Britain's Independence Day from 18 May to 21 April.

A just war

The aims of this war are not merely to increase economic growth and provide more families with jobs (although experience shows that it will). Nor are its aims to improve living standards and reduce social exclusion (although experience shows that this is the most likely outcome). A War of Independence is just because dependence is bad, and independence is good – good in itself. The overwhelming moral, political and economic arguments are in its favour. It is a necessary and just war.

> Independence Day will be a benchmark symbol, so that the people will always be able to assess: 'Are we going forwards or backwards?'

Independence Day – a new national holiday

In this war, Independence Day – the day of the year on which people stop working for the government and start working for themselves – will be declared a national holiday, the day when we celebrate our independence from the government's tax demands. Of course, many of those demands are legitimate. The challenge is to answer the original question: how to solve the terrible problem that the government never seems to have enough money to spend on good things like health and education, without taking away people's independence through ever-increasing taxes.

Independence Day will be a benchmark symbol, so that the people will always be able to assess: 'Are we going forwards or backwards?'

THE WAR OF INDEPENDENCE – A SIMPLE OBJECTIVE

Independence Day – a test of maturity

Before the last General Election, Tony Blair spoke of his desire to create a young, vibrant country. But if this Government continues to raise tax, Independence Day will retreat even further. On the Government's published plans, it will have moved from 15 May, its position in 1997, to 28 May in 2001: thirteen days in four years. Individuals' independence will have been further undermined. So while it may well desire a young country, this Government could end up treating us more and more like children.

Imagine a different vision: not of a 'young' country, but of a mature country, where individual people are trusted to take more of the decisions that determine how they live their lives. That is what is meant by independence.

A realistic, common sense approach

This paper does not propose cutting back the role of government where it is doing a good job. But it goes against the grain that government should give with one hand and take with another on the scale that it does. In 1948, payments that transferred money between individuals constituted just 4% of national income. Today, as we have already seen, the figure is 13%.

A higher initial Income Tax threshold is proposed. That will render unnecessary a significant proportion of these transfer payments. This alone could deliver over half of the objective of the War of Independence.

The remaining two-fifths could be achieved in several ways, according to political preference. For example, in a number of areas, there is scope for a transfer of economic decision-making from government to the individual – on the general principle that lower tax rates will enable individuals to relieve government of some of its present expenditures on their behalf. Not a reduction in spending overall, just a reduction of *government* spending in favour of *individual* spending.

The ultimate objective is to diminish the role of government by a fifth – from 37% of the economy to 30%, while enhancing the resources available for public health and education. The British people would then be able to celebrate their first victory in the War of Independence.

THE WAR OF INDEPENDENCE – A DECLARATION

Making possible a boost for health and education

The amount of money that the state spends on the public services people value most will be untouched: schools, the police and so on. But a radical approach, which involves redesigning the entire system of tax and spending, could facilitate a significant increase in the amount of money that is spent on health and education.

We need a political consensus

Calls for modernisation are not new. So the question that arises is: why has it never happened? There is one simple explanation. It is not because our political leaders are oblivious to the need: on the contrary, there is almost universal agreement about what the problems are, and the urgency of tackling them. Rather, a national culture has emerged which stops political leaders taking the required action. British politicians have become paralysed by fear of public reaction to fundamental reform of our system of tax and benefits. Every action that is proposed is always analysed in terms of winners and losers, short-term effects, precise calculations of personal financial advantage – and thereby political advantage. Unless we change our political culture, we will never change the dependency culture that has been inadvertently created. Agreement is needed that we are on the wrong path, and that we must change to a different one.

Fighting and winning the War of Independence will benefit whichever political party chooses to take up the challenge. It will help make that party more popular. It will lead to electoral success.

The key to electoral success in Britain

For many years there has been a direct correlation between voting intention and party ratings on 'tax' and 'managing the economy'. Figure 2.5 illustrates how a government's reputation for economic management is particularly important when a general election is due. By 1997, the incoming Labour Government was judged to have superior economic competence to that of the outgoing Conservative Government.

Most successful political parties have built their success on their economic management credentials. For many years, the Conservative critique of Labour was based on Labour's alleged inability to provide a strong economy. This is a longstanding theme of successful Conservative election campaigns.

THE WAR OF INDEPENDENCE – A SIMPLE OBJECTIVE

FIGURE 2.5 The Government and the Economy.

On balance do you agree or disagree that "in the long term, this Government's policies will improve the state of Britain's economy?

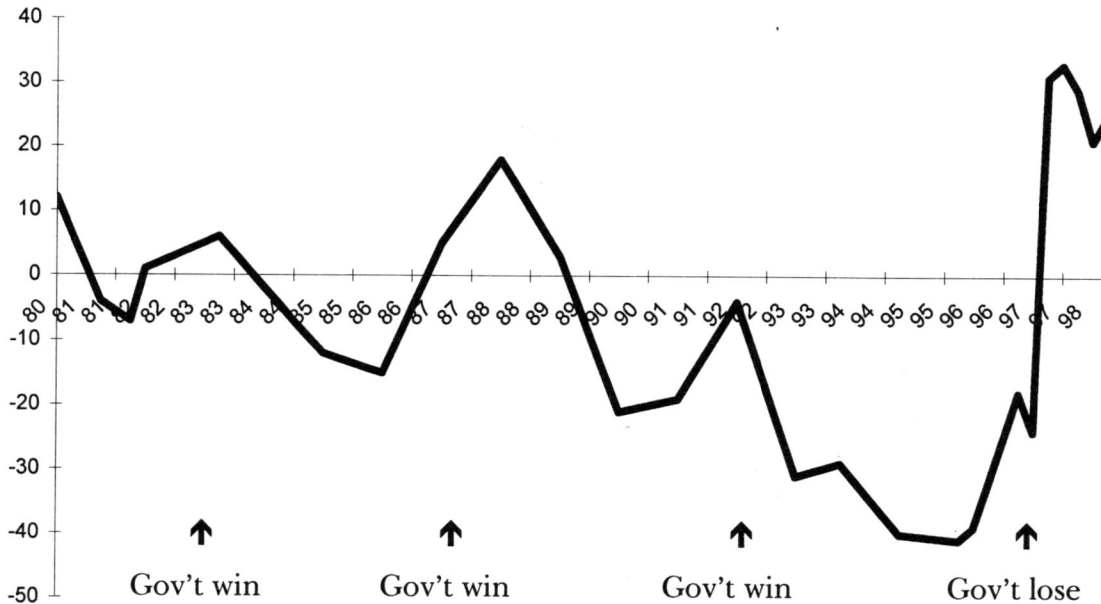

Source: MORI British Public Opinion

There is a straight line from the Conservative slogan: 'Post Office Savings in Danger' in the 1932 election, to 'Labour isn't Working' in the 1979 election, and 'Labour's Tax Bombshell' in 1992.

There is a consistent economic focus in Conservative campaigns: that while Labour spokesmen wore their hearts on their sleeves, and wanted the parade to slow down to the speed of the slowest participant, the Conservatives preferred a more hard-headed, practical approach to economic matters, best summed up by Iain MacLeod:

> *The Liberals may dream their dreams. And Labour may scheme their schemes.*
> *But we have work to do.*

A literal interpretation was that Conservatives knew how to look after your money and that Labour did not.

But the Conservative Party lost its economic credentials in Autumn 1992 when sterling was ejected from the Exchange Rate Mechanism. The depth of the recession in the early 1990s while sterling was in the ERM (and unable to lower its interest rates) made a large hole in the government's finances. This required the tax burden to be increased sharply soon after the economy emerged from recession, thus tarnishing the party's "low-tax" image (see figure 2.6). By 1997 'New Labour' were able to convince the British public that the economy was safe in their hands and that Income Tax rates would not be increased.

FIGURE 2.6 Political analysis of changes in overall taxation (as a % of GDP)

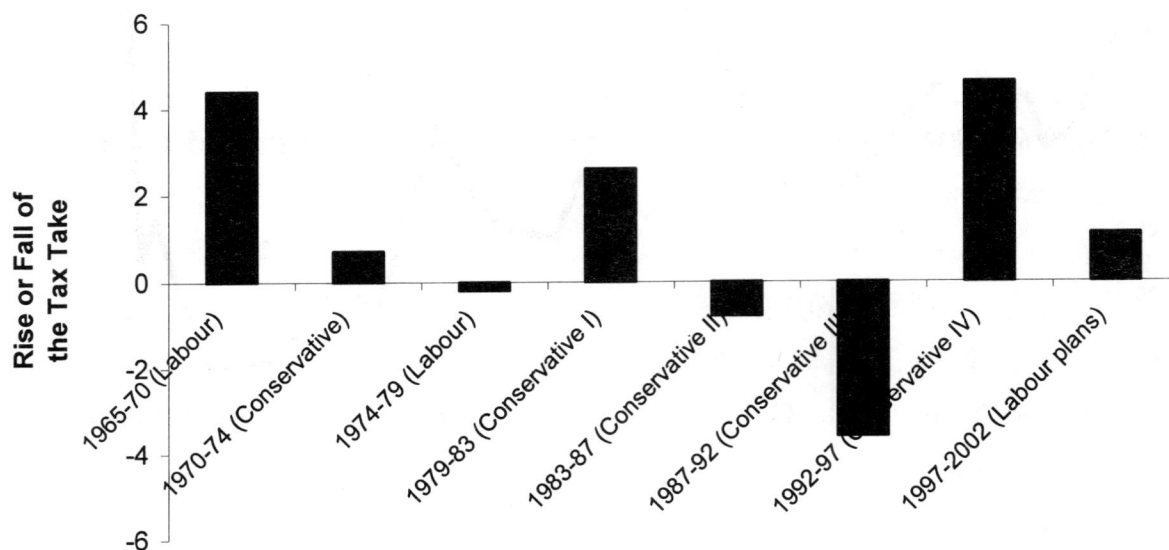

Sources: *Inland Revenue Statistics and the Pre-Budget Report, November 1998.*

The intellectual vice in which the Conservative Party was gripped in the 1997 election was entirely economic. Voters displayed textbook logic:

1. *The Conservatives have run the economy badly (ERM Exit; Tax Rises)....*
2. *and even if they could convince me they have run the economy well (Low Unemployment; Low Inflation etc)...*
3. *Labour will not ruin it (New, Reformed).*

Until the 1997 election, 'low tax' had been an important part of the Conservative Party's presentation of its economic case to the electorate.

This is ironic as Income Tax is a Tory invention. Income tax was first introduced by a Tory Prime Minister, Pitt the Younger. It was only abolished in 1816 by a backbench revolt against Liverpool's Tory Government, by radicals and Whigs led by

THE WAR OF INDEPENDENCE – A SIMPLE OBJECTIVE

the ultra-radical Henry Brougham who argued that Income Tax was 'an engine that should not be left at the disposal of extravagant ministers'.

Throughout the post war period, Conservatives were considered the low tax party, Labour the high tax party. When the Conservatives won four elections in a row, in the 70s, 80s and 90s, tax was a central issue. In exit polls, 'tax' was the number one 'reason for not voting Labour' when Labour lost the 1992 election.

Labour's pollster, Philip Gould, testifies to the power of taxation in the Conservative armoury when he writes of that election:

> On 12 December, I delivered the 1992 'War Book': the complete campaign for the election. I said our first weakness was tax, our second, lack of trust. The Tories' core message would be 'You can't trust Labour'. Their key attacks would be on tax... and the core themes would be Kinnock against Major and high-tax Labour against low-tax Conservatives. Less than four weeks after I wrote the War Book the Conservatives hit us on tax, with the 'Tax Bombshell' campaign on 6 January 1992. I was out of the country and heard the news over the telephone. As the news went on and on – National Insurance, top rate of tax, £1,000 per family – I knew we were finished. And less than three months later the Tories launched their election campaign, with the slogan 'You Can't Trust Labour'.

Today, 'tax' is the only issue where the Conservatives' poll ratings are even close to Labour's – a folk memory of other days. But the Conservative Party lost tax as its ace when New Labour leaders woke up and adopted a 'low tax' approach.

Because of this convergence of political attitudes to taxation, many people in both parties consider tax to have lost its potency as a political issue; that it is no longer a discriminator between the parties because Labour is now a 'prudent', 'low tax' party too. Is it true that tax is no longer a political issue in Britain?

The Conservative Party under Lady Thatcher put forward two arguments for low tax. The first was *moral*. It concerned 'freedom' and 'choice'. The idea was to leave people with more in their pocket, free to spend as they chose.

The second argument was *economic*. This was to do with 'incentives' and 'a bigger cake'. Lower tax, the Conservative Party argued, meant more incentives, so people worked harder, so they made a bigger cake, so everyone's share of the cake was bigger, so there was more to spend on the public services. The analogy was with the Good

Samaritan, who could only help because he had the money to do so. The logic was that 'caring that works costs cash' – in other words, good things had to be paid for by wealth creation. Ironically, Lady Thatcher said, lower taxes created more wealth overall because lower tax *rates* meant more tax *revenue*.

But in Britain today, many people say the moral argument for low tax has been tarnished by 'greed' and 'fat cats'. 'Low tax' is said to be a 1980s concept, 'out of touch' with the 'caring 90s'. Surveys seem to support this view. The percentage of British people who are ready to pay 'higher taxes for better public services' has doubled in a decade from 30% to 60%.

And many economists in Britain now say that while the economic argument for lower Income Tax applies from a 98% tax rate to a 40% rate, it does not have the same wealth-creating effect in reducing below 40%. So tax has dropped off the political agenda.

It is time to put it back on. But in a manner which reflects the sophistication and wariness of the modern British electorate. An informed proposal about the wider role of taxation and government spending will help any political party to win electoral respect. Radical proposals can excite the imagination. But the worst of all worlds would be a continuation of the *status quo* – for the electorate has grown weary of politicians' glib or pat answers to the complex and intractable problems of tax and spending.

CHAPTER THREE

THE EVOLUTION OF THE PRESENT SYSTEM OF TAX AND SPENDING

The financing of wars

FROM THE EARLIEST TIMES, governments have imposed taxes in order to finance military expenditures. Income tax was announced in 1798, and introduced exactly 200 years ago in 1799, as a means of paying for the war against Napoleon. William Pitt the Younger was Prime Minister and Chancellor of the Exchequer, and needed greater 'aid and contribution for the prosecution of the war'.

'Certain duties upon income' as outlined in the Act of 1799 were to be the temporary solution. Income tax was to be applied at a rate of 10% on the total income of the taxpayer. A short-lived peace treaty with Napoleon allowed Henry Addington, Pitt's successor, to repeal Income Tax. However, renewed fighting led to Addington's 1803 Act which set the pattern for Income Tax today.

The 1803 Act looked for a 'contribution of the profits arising from property, professions, trades and offices' (the words 'income tax' were deliberately avoided). It introduced two significant changes:

- taxation at source – the Bank of England would deduct Income Tax when paying interest to holders of gilts, for example; and,

- the division of Income Taxes into five 'Schedules' – A (income from land and buildings), B (farming profits), C (public annuities), D (self-employment and other items not covered by A, B, C or E) and E (salaries, annuities and pensions).

Income tax changed little under various Chancellors, contributing to the war effort up to the Battle of Waterloo in 1815. The following year, Income Tax was abolished and Parliament decided that all documents related to it should be pulped.

THE WAR OF INDEPENDENCE – A DECLARATION

However, by 1842, the Treasury's coffers were depleted once more and Income Tax was revived. There followed a long list of Prime Ministers who vowed to abolish it, but none of them succeeded. Between the Crimean War and the Great Depression of the 1880s, Income Tax receded in significance, supplying only £6 million of the government's £77 million revenue in 1874. Customs and Excise duties contributed the largest share of tax revenue, at £47 million.

From war to welfare

With the formation of a new government by the Liberals following the 1905 election came a change in the way taxation was viewed – from a means of paying for wars to a way of supporting the welfare of the people. The structural dependence on the taxation of personal income and expenditure that is evident in today's fiscal system was already in place by 1908; the main development during the past 80 years has been the replacement of the taxation of personal wealth by the taxation of corporate incomes, as shown in figure 3.1.

A change in the way taxation was viewed: from a means of paying for wars to a way of supporting the welfare of the people.

In 1908, the Chancellor of the Exchequer, Lloyd George, introduced non-contributory old-age pensions, and – in the 'People's Budget' of 1909 – plans for a tax on property values. The rejection of this Bill by the House of Lords led to the 1911 Parliament Act which removed the Lords' power of veto.

By 1914, the standard rate of Income Tax was 6%, and the tax raised from Income Tax and super-tax was £47 million. By 1918 – again to pay for war – the standard rate had jumped to 30%, realising £294 million a year including super-tax (although tax allowances had also been increased in order to ease the burden for those on low incomes). In addition, an Excess Profits Duty was introduced as a device to deny companies the opportunity to derive exceptional profits from the war effort. At that time, corporate taxation was not normally a significant source of revenue for the Exchequer and did not become so again until the 1960s.

Learning from the lessons in 1914, the outbreak of the Second World War saw immediate action to raise revenue for the war effort. 'Finance is the fourth arm of

THE EVOLUTION OF THE PRESENT SYSTEM

defence', said Chancellor Sir John Simon in the first War Budget. In 1939, the standard rate of Income Tax was 29% with surtax at 41%. Ten million people were liable for tax, and the total sum raised was £400 million. By 1944-45 successive increases in rates and lowering of allowances meant there were 14 million taxpayers and nearly £1,400 million raised.

FIGURE 3.1 Long-term development of the UK tax structure 1908-1998

Year	Total tax take	Income taxes on individuals (£ millions)	%	Expenditure taxes (£ millions)	%	Company taxes (£ millions)	%	Wealth taxes on individuals (£ millions)	%
1908-09	127	34	26.8	65	49.6	2	1.6	26	20.5
1918-19	786	294	37.5	162	20.7	287	36.6	43	5.5
1928-29	664	293	44.1	257	38.7	3	0.5	111	16.7
1938-39	898	399	44.5	377	42.1	24	2.7	98	10.9
1948-49	3,665	1,460	39.8	1,610	43.9	360	9.8	235	6.4
1958-59	5,310	2,484	46.7	2,298	43.2	275	5.2	253	4.8
1968-69	12,903	4,574	35.5	4,994	38.7	2,782	21.6	553	4.3
1978-79	40,916	18,763	45.8	14,948	36.5	6,050	12.9	1,155	2.8
1988-89	121,382	43,433	35.8	52,376	43.2	19,925	16.4	5,649	4.7
1998-99	226,300	84,300	37.3	100,200	44.3	33,100	14.6	8,700	3.8

Source: Inland Revenue Statistics 1998

The growth of the Welfare State

The 50 or so years since the end of World War II have seen greater social and economic changes than any other comparable period. The National Health Service was introduced in 1948. The phrase 'Welfare State' began to be used to reflect a wide range of social provisions including broader national insurance provisions, the introduction of child allowances, the raising of the school-leaving age and increased old-age pensions.

From 1945 to 1965, the UK economy enjoyed a virtually uninterrupted expansion of GDP per head, spurred initially by the reconstruction of towns and cities that were devastated by war. During this time, many industries were under public ownership and control and roughly 20% of government expenditure was on capital investment. Once the war had ceased to absorb additional resources, the government's current expenditures fell back to around 30% of GDP. The low rate of unemployment and the relatively small proportion of 'old age pensioners' helped to keep down the cost of national insurance and other benefits.

THE WAR OF INDEPENDENCE – A DECLARATION

In 1948-49, the total of all social security benefits was £471 million, representing under 4% of GDP. Retirement pensions, war pensions and widows' benefits amounted to £278 million, assistance to families £60 million, benefits to the unemployment and needy £78 million, the sick and disabled £44 million and all other benefits £11 million. By 1965-66, social security benefits had already assumed greater importance, at 6.3% of GDP, but pensions and widows' benefits still accounted for almost two-thirds of the total. This share had fallen to 36% by 1994-95 as unemployment, invalidity and housing benefits rose to prominence.

Figure 3.2 shows that 1976-77 was the climax for the share of total government spending in the economy; very nearly 50% of national expenditure was under the direction of the public sector. Strenuous efforts to scale back the influence of government during the late-1970s, prompted by the IMF's intervention in 1976, were frustrated by the slide into economic recession during 1980. Nevertheless, a significant reduction in the size of the public sector occurred in the second half of the decade. The share of total managed expenditure fell below 40% and has returned to this level again in recent years. However, almost all of this is current expenditure; after the large-scale privatisations of the 1980s and 1990s, net investment by the public sector is minimal.

FIGURE 3.2 Government spending as a % of the size of the economy

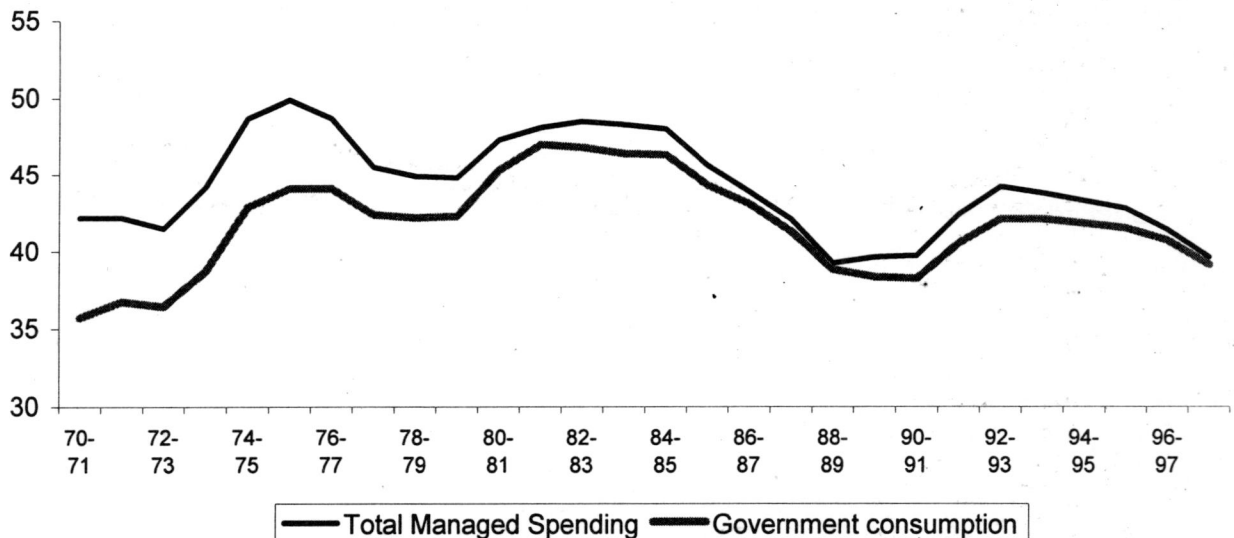

Sources: Comprehensive Spending Review, Cm 4011, July 1988 and Pre-Budget Report, Cm 4076, November 1998.

The composition of public expenditure between the various departments and agencies has altered most in respect of social security payments. Figure 3.3 illustrates the transformation of the payments share from 20% in 1970-71 to about 36% today. By contrast, expenditures on health and education have changed little during the past 20 years. These budgets have increased in real terms, but scarcely in relation to the total government budget. (See figure 3.4.)

FIGURE 3.3 Social Security payments as a share of total government expenditure

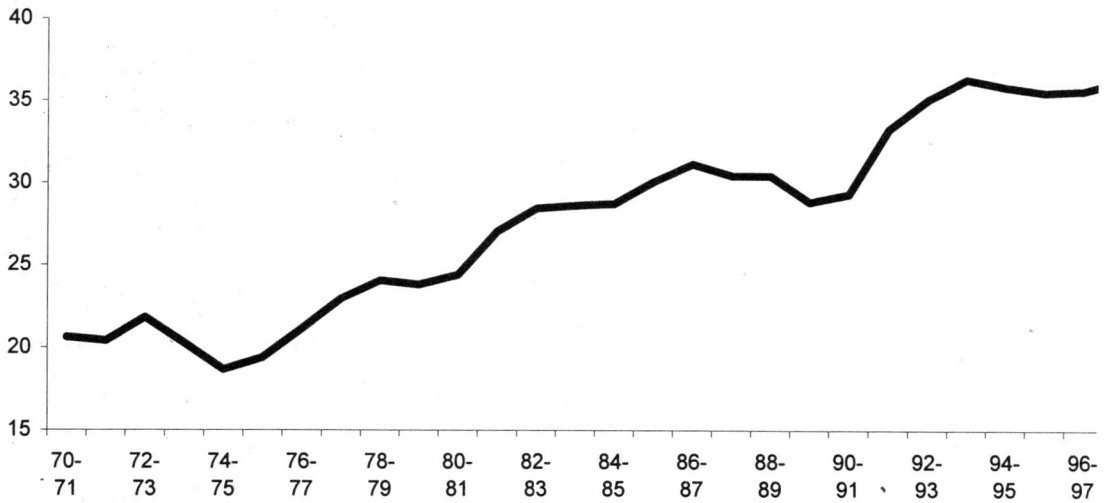

Source: Datastream.

FIGURE 3.4 Share of health and education spending in total UK Government expenditure

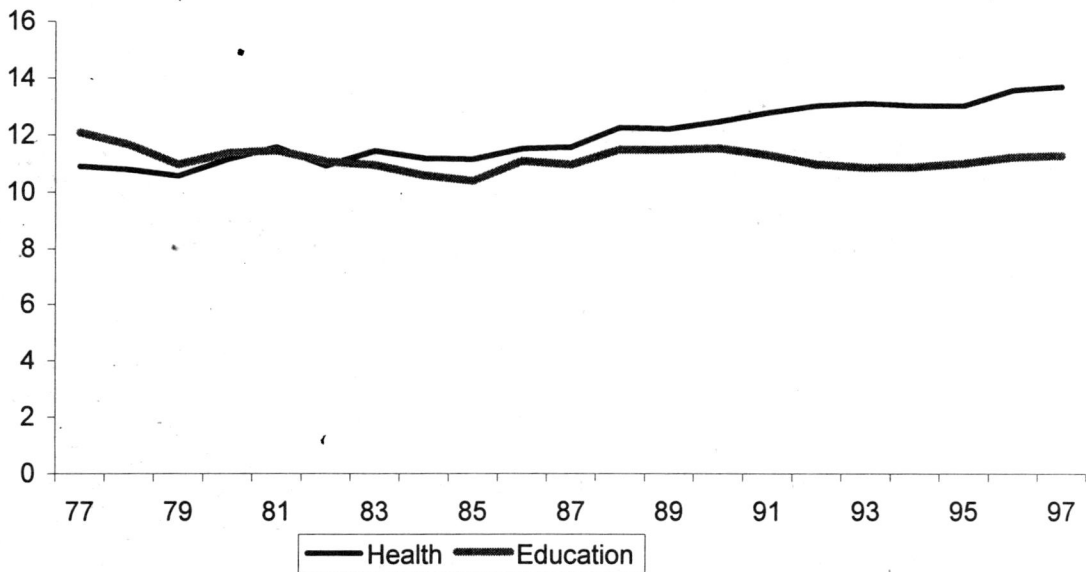

Source: Datastream.

THE WAR OF INDEPENDENCE – A DECLARATION

Balancing the budget

During the 1950s and 1960s, the UK government's budget was broadly balanced. Tax revenue and other recurrent income (such as rents and surpluses) was sufficient to cover all expenditures, averaged out over a period of 5 or 10 years. In contrast, deficits averaged between 2% and 2.5% of GDP throughout the 1970s and 1980s, only to explode in the aftermath of the 1990s recession to 7.8% of GDP in 1993. Since then, the budget has been brought under control and the 1998-99 fiscal year yielded a small surplus. However, vast public debts have been accumulated in the past 30 years and these must still be serviced. Debt interest currently absorbs about 3.5% of GDP, equivalent to 8% of all government spending.

Some comparisons with other countries

It is important to appreciate that the expansion of government, and the associated tax burden required to finance it, has been even more obvious in other developed countries than in the UK. The OECD's Revenue Statistics cover the period from 1965 to 1995,

FIGURE 3.5 Tax as a % of GDP

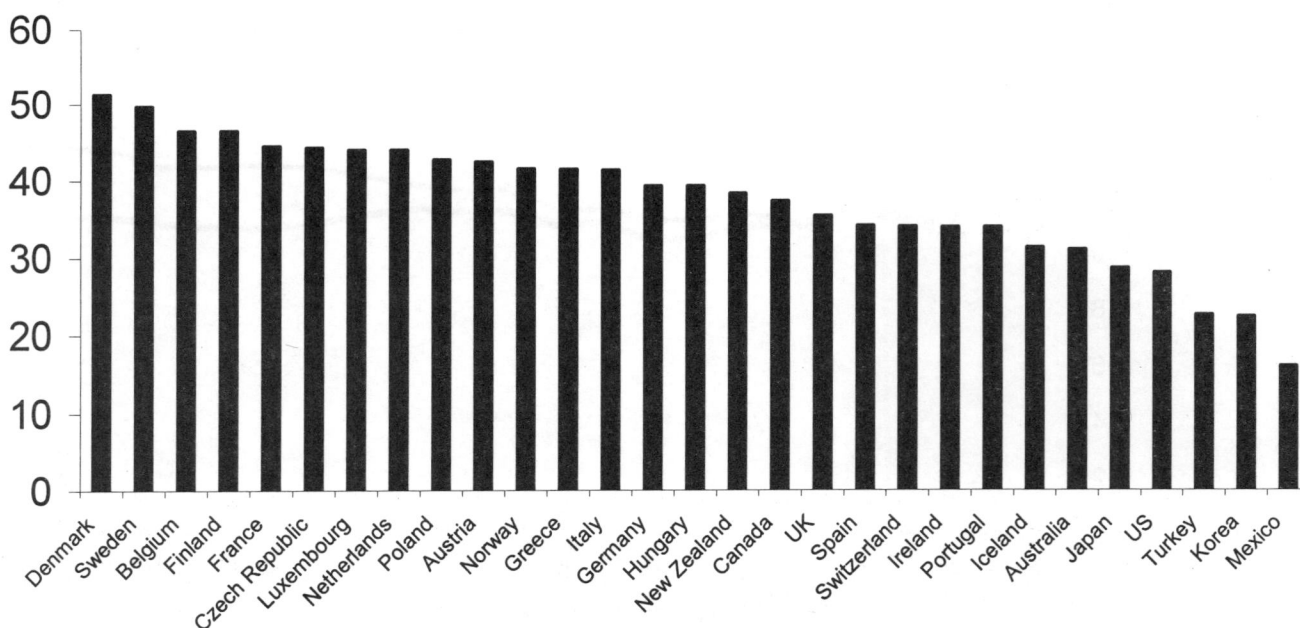

Source: OECD Revenue Statistics, 1997 edition

during which the average ratio of tax revenue to GDP has risen from 26.1% to 37.4%. For the UK, the growth was from 30.4% to 35.3% over the same period. The most extreme example is Sweden, whose ratio climbed from 35% in 1965 to a peak of 55.6% in 1990, before falling back to 49.7% in 1995. Other countries have resisted the trend towards larger government more successfully: the USA's ratio rose only from 24.3% to 27.9% over the 30-year period.

The dynamic effect of a low tax burden on an economy is illustrated by the United States. The US government taxes only 27.9% of national income. But instead of finding this insufficient to meet its spending needs, it is expected that the US economy will generate a healthy budget surplus over the next 10 years.

> **The US government taxes only 27.9% of national income. But it is expected that the US economy will generate a healthy budget surplus over the next 10 years.**

Figures 3.6 and 3.7 contrast the relative importance of the different types of taxation in the various countries. Income taxes of all kinds account for just 7% of GDP in Mexico and 9% of GDP in the Korean Republic and Turkey, rising to 36% of GDP in Sweden.

FIGURE 3.6 All forms of income taxation as a % of GDP

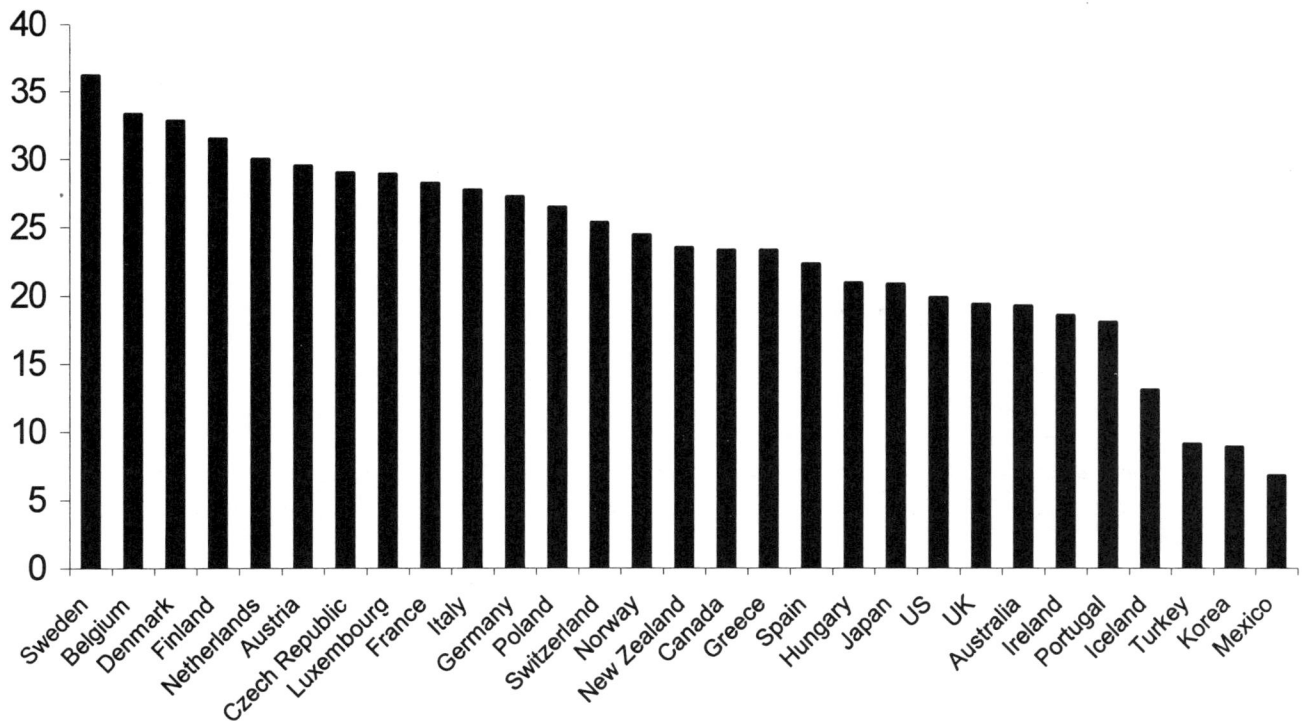

Source OECD Revenue Statistics, 1997 edition

Expenditure taxes are most onerous in Hungary, at 17.5% of GDP, and the least burdensome in Japan (4.2%) and the USA (5%).

FIGURE 3.7 Expenditure taxes as a % of GDP

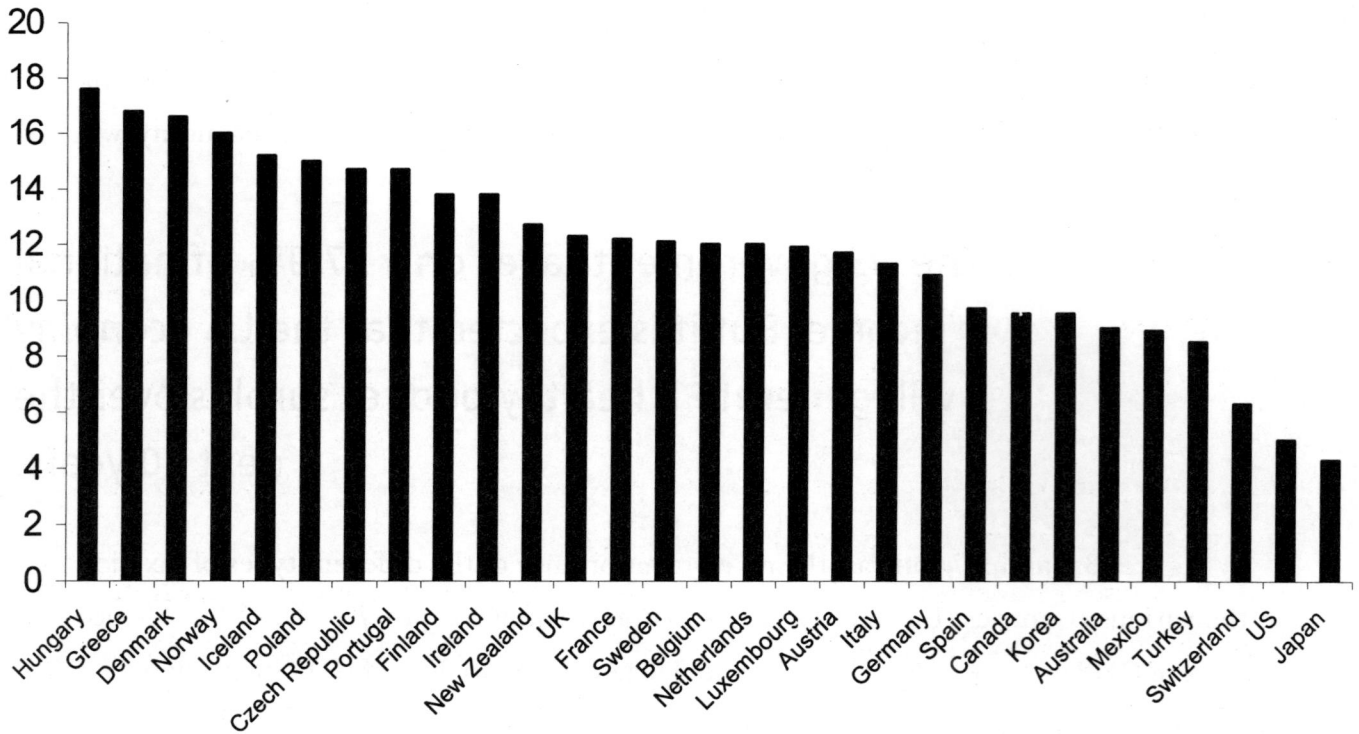

CHAPTER FOUR

ECONOMIC ARGUMENTS FOR THE WAR

THE ECONOMIC ARGUMENTS FOR a modest government sector and for low tax rates are straightforward and well-known. Excessive government interference in the production process or the pricing mechanism creates distortion and inefficiency, lowering the potential size and growth of the whole economy. High tax rates discriminate against productive citizens and subtract wealth from taxpayers without providing them with any compensating increase in government services.

Yet these arguments are difficult to prove: empirical studies in numerous individual countries have laboured to establish their validity. There are so many variables that are beyond experimental control that it is difficult to disentangle the various economic effects.

However, cross-country comparisons offer a more promising approach. For more than a decade the Fraser Institute in Vancouver has organised the development of a comprehensive framework of measurement for economic freedom. They define the core ingredients of economic freedom as personal choice, the protection of private property and the freedom of individuals to enter into trading contracts. Thanks to the efforts of a network of 47 economic institutes around the world, a comprehensive and comparable list of 25 measures of economic independence has been devised for 119 countries.

FIGURE 4.1 Components of the Index of Economic Freedom

Broad heading	Weight (%)
Size of Government	11.0
Structure of the economy and use of markets	14.2
Monetary policy and price stability	9.2
Freedom of access to alternative currencies	14.6
Security of property rights and viability of contracts	16.6
Freedom to trade with foreigners	17.1
Freedom of exchange in capital and financial markets	17.2
Total	**100.0**

Source: J. Gwartney and R. Lawson, Economic Freedom of the World: 1998/99 Interim Report (Vancouver, B.C.: The Fraser Institute)

The summary rating of each country has been derived by weighting together the various measures, including those derived from continuous series such as the annual inflation rate and the share of government consumption in total spending and scored variables such as the risk of confiscation of private property and the extent of interest rate controls and regulations. The measures are arranged under seven broad headings as shown in figure 4.1.

Argument 1: Countries with the highest scores for economic independence tend to have the highest standards of living and those with the lowest scores are among the poorest in the world

All governments exert a degree of influence over the economic behaviour of individuals. There are three main ways in which this may be achieved: first, by direct ownership and control of the means of production; second, through high taxes and extensive transfers of resources between individuals; third, by interference in the pricing mechanism for goods, labour and capital. In these various ways, government can take an active or passive role in deciding the industrial structure of the economy, the range of goods and services that are produced and consumed, the means of distribution, the prices to be paid for goods and services and the rewards for human effort.

The overwhelming conclusion is that individual prosperity is considerably greater in liberalised economies.

At one extreme is the command economy and national plan, where the agents of government take all the decisions over resource allocation. At the other extreme is the laissez-faire economy in which the government fulfils only a bare minimum of functions, such as the preservation of law and order, leaving the private sector to determine the structure of the economy, the levels of employment and average incomes. On the assumption that most government spending will be financed from taxes on current incomes and expenditures, it follows that the greater the degree of influence and direction that the state exerts over the economy, then higher will be the tax burden on individuals.

At a secondary level, the government is also able to influence private behaviour through different types of taxation, and the relationship between the tax burden and an individual's income or wealth. The rate of deduction of tax from income can have a profound effect on the attractiveness of additional hours of work that people will willingly supply.

ECONOMIC ARGUMENTS FOR THE WAR

Figures 4.2 and 4.3 contrast the living standards of the top 20 and bottom 20 countries with respect to the degree of economic independence in each country. While there is a sprinkling of anomalies, the overwhelming conclusion is that individual prosperity is considerably greater in liberalised economies.

FIGURE 4.2 Top 20 rated-countries and their average living standards (GDP per capita)

Country	Economic Freedom rating (scored out of 10)	GDP per capita (1996, US$)	World rank
Hong Kong	9.6	24,290	13
Singapore	9.4	30,550	5
New Zealand	9.2	15,720	21
USA	9.1	28,020	8
UK	9.0	19,600	17
Canada	8.8	19,020	18
Argentina	8.7	8,380	27
Netherlands	8.6	25,940	11
Panama	8.6	3,080	43
Australia	8.6	20,090	15
Ireland	8.6	17,110	19
Switzerland	8.5	44,350	1
Japan	8.3	40,940	2
Denmark	8.3	32,100	4
Norway	8.3	34,510	3
Belgium	8.2	26,440	9
El Salvador	8.2	1,700	58
Finland	8.2	23,240	14
Germany	8.2	28,870	6
France	8.1	26,270	10

Sources: J. Gwartney and R. Lawson, *Economic Freedom of the World: 1998/99 Interim Report* (Vancouver, B.C.: The Fraser Institute), *World Development Report* (Washington D.C. : World Bank, 1998)

FIGURE 4.3 Worst 20 rated-countries and their average living standards (GDP per capita)

Country	Economic Freedom rating (scored out of 10)	GDP per capita (1996, US$)	World rank
Guinea-Bissau	3.1	250	115
Congo, Dem. Rep.	3.2	130	128
Rwanda	3.5	190	123
Albania	4.1	820	80
Sierra Leone	4.1	200	122
Malawi	4.1	180	124
Romania	4.2	1,600	62
Madagascar	4.2	250	116
Algeria	4.2	1,520	63
Central African Republic	4.2	310	107
Ukraine	4.2	1,200	68
Togo	4.4	300	110
Bangladesh	4.4	260	114
Congo Republic	4.5	670	83
Nigeria	4.6	240	118
Syria	4.7	1,160	71
Benin	4.7	350	104
Nepal	4.8	210	120
Burundi	4.8	170	125
Chad	4.8	160	127

Sources: J. Gwartney and R. Lawson, *Economic Freedom of the World: 1998/99 Interim Report* (Vancouver, B.C.: The Fraser Institute), *World Development Report* (Washington D.C. : World Bank, 1998)

THE WAR OF INDEPENDENCE – A DECLARATION

Which countries have made the most progress in the 1990s?
A previous report from the Fraser Institute in 1997, noted the strong association of high economic independence ratings not only with high per capita GDP, but also with stronger growth in living standards over the previous decade. While correlation does not prove causality, the circumstantial evidence backs up the statistics. Countries that were once racked by inflation, corruption and political turmoil have laid the foundations for economic stability and sustainable growth. The most dramatic transformations of the 1990s have been in Latin America, notably in Peru and Argentina.

Argument 2: Countries in which government spending forms a large proportion of total consumption of goods and services suffer a slower pace of economic growth than those in which government spending represents a small proportion
Whenever governments take decisions about the composition of goods and services to be produced, either through the ownership of industries and capital assets or through placing orders with privately owned enterprises, there is a potential conflict with the pattern of consumption that individuals would have chosen themselves. Certain facilities and utilities (such as roads, bridges and an impartial police force) may demand a high degree of centralisation in their provision. However, beyond the realm of public goods, governments around the world have made very different choices about the control of other types of economic activity. Figure 4.4 contrasts the recent economic performance of three groups of 10 countries that have taken markedly different decisions about the scope of government consumption.

> It is difficult to locate a single example of a country with a large government sector displaying consistently strong economic growth.

The results are striking in terms of their uniformity, despite the use of developed and developing countries with very different income levels and political structures. It is difficult to locate a single example of a country with a large government sector displaying consistently strong economic growth. Ireland, with a government consumption share of 21.1% and average GDP growth of 6.6% is the closest. However, Ireland is not a large country and it has been favoured in the allocation of resources within the European Community. It would be dangerous to generalise from the Irish example.

ECONOMIC ARGUMENTS FOR THE WAR

At the opposite extreme, tier 3 comprises 10 nations from Asia and Latin America with a total population of 550 million. Some have endured serious economic crises during the 1990s and yet have rebounded strongly. The recent traumas in South East Asia offer another opportunity to observe the dynamism with which unencumbered nations are able to recover from their setbacks. Countries with large government sectors rarely manage a 4% economic growth rate in any year.

FIGURE 4.4 General government consumption expenditures as a percentage of total consumption versus the average pace of economic growth between 1989 and 1997

Country	Government consumption Share in total (%)	Average GDP growth 1989-1997, %p.a.
Tier 1		
Sweden	33.4	0.9
Denmark	31.8	2.3
Czech Republic	30.7	-1.5
Finland	28.9	0.8
Germany	25.6	2.4
Austria	25.6	2.3
South Africa	25.0	1.0
Canada	25.0	1.6
France	24.7	1.5
UK	24.3	1.5
Tier 1 average	**27.5**	**1.3**
Tier 2		
Taiwan	19.3	6.4
Colombia	19.1	4.0
Netherlands	18.9	2.7
New Zealand	18.8	2.3
Belgium	18.7	1.7
Singapore	18.0	8.3
Korean Rep.	17.2	7.4
Greece	16.9	1.5
Thailand	15.7	7.6
Bolivia	15.6	4.1
Tier 2 average	**17.8**	**4.6**
Tier 3		
Pakistan	14.3	4.7
Chile	13.2	7.1
Mexico	13.2	2.7
Argentina	12.6	5.3
Hong Kong	12.5	5.1
Sri Lanka	12.4	5.2
Indonesia	11.1	7.6
Peru	10.2	4.1
Paraguay	8.7	2.9
Venezuela	8.6	3.1
Tier 3 average	**11.7**	**4.8**

Sources: J. Gwartney and R. Lawson, Economic Freedom of the World: 1998/99 Interim Report (Vancouver, B.C.: The Fraser Institute), OECD Economic Outlook, June 1998 and IMF International Financial Statistics Yearbook 1998

Argument 3: Countries in which transfer payments and subsidies form a large fraction of GDP grow more slowly than those in which these payments are minimal
A feature of the large western developed economies is the extensive range of transfers that the governments make between individuals. State-organised welfare benefits and

pensions, and subsidies to enfeebled industries, are easy to institute and increase. But they are troublesome to withdraw or reduce. Many governments have tried to limit transfer payments only to abandon their plans in the face of intense lobbying. The line of least political resistance has been to increase taxation instead of curtailing the welfare system. However, there are dozens of countries throughout the world that do not have even a rudimentary welfare system, let alone a cradle-to-grave version. Once again, it is instructive to compare the recent performance of countries with differing attributes.

FIGURE 4.5 Transfers and subsidies as a percentage of GDP versus the average pace of economic growth between 1989 and 1997

Country	Transfers and subsidies Share in GDP (%)	Average GDP growth 1989-1997, %p.a.
Tier 1		
Sweden	32.8	0.9
Italy	29.4	1.2
Netherlands	29.1	2.7
Czech Republic	28.6	-1.5
France	28.4	1.5
Denmark	26.5	2.3
Belgium	26.3	1.7
Austria	25.2	2.3
Greece	24.6	1.5
Poland	24.4	1.5
Tier 1 average	**27.5**	**1.4**
Tier 2		
Switzerland	18.9	0.5
Spain	18.9	2.0
Ireland	18.8	6.6
UK	17.7	1.5
Canada	17.7	1.6
Brazil	14.9	1.9
Turkey	14.6	4.4
Australia	14.4	2.7
USA	14.1	2.2
Portugal	13.4	2.3
Tier 2 average	**16.3**	**2.6**
Tier 3		
Taiwan	5.9	6.4
Mexico	5.5	2.7
Malaysia	4.7	8.7
Korean Rep.	3.6	7.4
Pakistan	2.7	4.7
Singapore	1.8	8.3
Indonesia	1.6	7.6
Hong Kong	1.1	5.1
Thailand	1.0	7.6
Philippines	0.7	3.1
Tier 3 average	**2.9**	**6.2**

Sources: J. Gwartney and R. Lawson, Economic Freedom of the World: 1998/99 Interim Report (Vancouver, B.C.: The Fraser Institute), OECD Economic Outlook, June 1998 and IMF International Financial Statistics Yearbook 1998

The evidence in figure 4.5 suggests that the extent of the transfer payments system is even more significant for economic dynamism than the share of government consumption in the economy. Where a network of benefits and privileges supports a large section of the population, economic incentives are eroded and the implied level of overall taxation is correspondingly high. Figure 4.6 compares the deduction rates of tax and social contributions from the income of a sole earner family and figure 4.7 contrasts the standard rate of VAT in various European countries.

FIGURE 4.6 Deductions for tax and compulsory social contributions as percentage of gross salary for a married man with 2 dependent children, based on an annual salary of US$ 75,000

Country	Deductions (%)
Belgium	59.6
Germany	58.5
Finland	48.9
Sweden	48.3
Denmark	46.8
Spain	44.1
Netherlands	42.5
Luxembourg	42.5
Ireland	41.9
Portugal	40.9
Greece	38.1
Italy	37.9
Austria	33.0
UK	30.0

Source: European Union Business Investment Report, 1998

FIGURE 4.7 Standard rates of Value Added Tax in the European Union

Country	Rate (%)
Denmark	25.0
Sweden	25.0
Finland	22.0
Ireland	21.0
Belgium	21.0
Austria	20.0
Italy	19.0
France	18.6
Greece	18.0
Netherlands	17.5
UK	17.5
Portugal	17.0
Germany	16.0
Spain	16.0
Luxembourg	15.0

Source: European Union Business Investment Report, 1998

These comparisons are also indicative of a negative relationship between government size and full employment, and between high tax rates and full employment. Very low marginal deduction rates seem also to be associated with rapid growth of income per head. The more general result is that across nations of all sizes and living standards, irrespective of any particular point in their business cycle, countries whose citizens are the most independent from state interference tend to have faster rates of economic growth and to generate more employment. This is the principal economic argument for waging war on excessive government involvement.

CHAPTER FIVE

AN AGENDA FOR REFORM

THE REFORMING AGENDA OF THE 1980S consisted of privatisation and liberalisation – the transfer of ownership and control of utilities and industrial corporations from the public sector to the private sector, and the elimination of cartels, monopolies and restrictive practices. Twenty years on, a new political consensus has formed that acknowledges the beneficial effects of these reforms for the British economy; there are few who would seek to reverse them. Indeed, Tony Blair's New Labour has its own modest privatisation plans and has revitalised the flagging Private Finance Initiative under which many public buildings, roads and amenities will be constructed in future.

The true battleground for reform at the start of the 21st century is not the National Health Service or the education system, but the tax and welfare payments system. Until the UK embraces a fundamental reform of its transfer payments mechanism, it will stagger under the weight of an ever-increasing tax burden and will struggle to make adequate resources available to public health or education. If opinion polls are any guide, there is enormous public support for the reallocation of government expenditures towards front-line healthcare and primary and secondary education. Yet this transformation has proved elusive even for a Government with a massive parliamentary majority.

The true battleground for reform at the start of the 21st century is the tax and welfare payments system.

Incremental reform of the existing tax, national insurance and benefit systems over the past 30 years has created a highly complex and contradictory framework of transfer payments. All attempts to unravel the wasteful and unintended features of the transfer system – such as the unemployment and poverty traps – have been half-hearted and piecemeal. In 1999, the problems loom as large as ever and the human and financial costs of large scale benefit dependency are still escalating.

AN AGENDA FOR REFORM

The current system of taxation and transfer payments is a horse designed by a committee which has been in standing session for 200 years. The outcome is an ungainly beast of burden. The time is ripe for fundamental reform.

> The current system of taxation and transfer payments is a horse designed by a committee which has been in standing session for 200 years. The outcome is an ungainly beast of burden.

A new agenda

Three elements require further consideration in a detailed research exercise:

1   **A reduction of the role of government in transferring incomes between individuals.**

2   **Exchanging the current mass of complex allowances for a lower tax burden.**

3   **Integration of the government departments that deal with transfers.**

These three changes, all detailed below, offer the scope to reduce the UK tax burden from over 37% of GDP to around 33% – the first steps towards bringing forward Independence Day from 18 May to 21 April each year. They will invigorate the economy, restore work incentives to those on low incomes and improve the underlying pace of economic growth.

In addition to a dramatic increase in personal independence, these bold measures would release resources to finance an increase in spending on health and education.

A reduction in the role of government in transferring incomes between individuals

This fundamental reform of the tax and benefit system would enable cash payments from the government to be exchanged for protection from Income Tax payments to the government, thus reversing the trend of the past 30 years. A substantial restoration of the real value of the personal Income Tax threshold would be funded by the matched withdrawal of benefits currently paid to working households. Millions of benefit and pension supplements (or top-ups) would become redundant. In addition, occupational pensioners could elect to receive all or part of their state pension as a tax credit.

THE WAR OF INDEPENDENCE – A DECLARATION

In the tax year 1998-99, there were 26.1 million individual taxpayers (the largest ever total). Back in 1958-59, there were only about 21 million. The main reason for this growth was that married couples with children received much larger tax allowances, lifting millions of them out of the tax system. The break-even point – defined as the value of earnings at which Income Tax paid is equal to the money received via a tax allowance or child benefit – was equal to more than 80% of average earnings (for all occupations) in 1960 as compared to 47.7% in 1997-98.

A single person earning 50% of the average for all adults in full-time employment currently loses 13.2% of their income in tax. A married man claiming the married couple's allowance loses 10.7% of his income. These proportions rise only to 18.1% for a single person and 16.8% for a married man on average earnings and to 20.9% and 20.1%, respectively, at the level of 150% of average earnings.

Splitting Income Tax payers into the richer and poorer halves of the distribution, the richer half pays 88% of personal Income Tax. The 7.6 million lower rate taxpayers contributed £4.4 billion of Income Tax in 1997-98, equivalent to just over 5% of gross tax payments. After deduction of tax credits (eg for mortgage interest relief), this falls to £3.8 billion – or less than 5% of net tax payments. In fact, 14.2 million individual taxpayers had total annual incomes of less than £10,000 in 1998-99, with total gross tax liabilities of £14.3 billion. With the introduction of tax credits, these liabilities are already being reduced to £12.6 billion.

A wholesale reform to raise the initial tax threshold – encompassing national insurance contributions as well as Income Tax – would not only bring a drastic reduction in the number of taxpayers, it would also eliminate millions of small payments by various government agencies to individuals.

Most working individuals with annual incomes below approximately £15,000 would simply cease to be taxpayers. Hardly any Income Tax payers aged over 65 would remain.

A radical reform of the tax and benefit system, so that the total starting income threshold for Income Tax and National Insurance payments was raised to about £15,000 per annum, would result in a loss of tax and National Insurance revenue of between £30 billion and £40 billion under the present system. In principle, it should be possible to cancel out an equivalent value of cash payments of benefits and pensions, without withdrawing support from individuals and families who are genuinely dependent. In the first instance, this reform would be strictly revenue-neutral, entailing a parallel reduction in cash-paid benefits and Income Tax receipts. However, in time it should be expected to improve the efficiency of the economy and to raise the underlying pace of GDP growth.

> ## People would typically receive benefits or pensions, or pay Income Tax; but seldom both at the same time.

By implication, most working individuals with annual incomes below approximately £15,000 would simply cease to be taxpayers. Hardly any Income Tax payers aged over 65 would remain. Social security benefits would continue to be paid to able-bodied people who are out of work but seeking employment. For those working part-time or in low paid jobs, the range of income over which social security benefits are phased out would no longer overlap with the threshold for payment of Income Tax. By separating the ranges of benefit withdrawal and Income Tax payment, the problem of very high marginal deduction rates would be greatly diminished. People would typically receive benefits or pensions, or pay Income Tax; but seldom both at the same time.

Exchanging the current mass of complex allowances for a lower tax burden
Under the present system, the government has the capacity to levy gross tax charges on companies and individuals amounting to a staggering 53% of GDP. Taxpayers are obliged to navigate a web of allowances, reliefs, and exemptions in order to claim back 16% of national income, bringing the net tax take to 37% of GDP. Apart from the expense and intrusion of such an arrangement, this system allows too much scope for 'hidden' tax increases whereby the impact of 'tax increases' is diluted by being presented as alterations to allowances. Thus, GDP continues to creep up imperceptibly.

A detailed study of an alternative, simplified system is needed, in which the web of allowances is simply exchanged for lower tax, by raising the starting threshold for Income Tax. The result would be a dramatically more transparent and open system, comprehensible to all.

Integration of the government departments that deal with transfers

A number of other advantages would flow from this radical rearrangement of the tax and benefits system. The administration of personal Income Tax by the Inland Revenue would be merged with the Department of Social Security and the Benefits and Contributions Agencies, allowing a comprehensive pooling of tax, contribution, benefit and pension data. The recurring costs of administering the system would fall dramatically due to the simplification of tax allowances and the elimination of duplicated tax assessments and benefit payments. The combined caseload of these offices could be reduced by 20% to 30%, perhaps more.

A dramatically more transparent and open system, comprehensible to all.

The integration of tax, National Insurance, benefit and pension records would also improve the detection of benefit fraud. A deliberate structural break in the administration of benefit payments would purge the longstanding abuses of the system. For example, by re-registering the National Insurance numbers of all adults, redundant numbers could be deleted from the system and any payments to them discontinued. This could yield far greater savings than costly and socially divisive snooping initiatives. A further reduction in the cost of fraudulent claims could be achieved by introducing "smart" National Insurance cards to replace benefit order books and electronic transfers to replace giro cheques. Social Security Secretary Alastair Darling highlighted the importance of cutting down the "manipulation and forging" of order books and giro cheques in a speech on 1 December 1998. Today's payments security technology is more than capable of rising to this challenge.

The annual savings from this reorganisation and rationalisation of the tax and payments system, coupled with a sharp reduction in benefit fraud, could release £5 billion of extra funding for health and education. However, there would also be dynamic gains from such a thorough overhaul of the system. Not least, the higher starting threshold for Income Tax should be expected to restore earnings incentives and promote employment and GDP growth.

In conclusion

Figure 5.1 provides an illustration of the possible impact of these three proposals outlined above. A detailed research exercise would aim to define the optimum simplification of the system.

FIGURE 5.1 Source of planned reductions in public expenditure and taxation

1997-98 values	Actual £ billion	Proposed £ billion	Difference £ billion	% of GDP
Reduction in public expenditure				
Proposal				
1 Savings from reduction in overlapping cash payments	105.2	70.2	-35.0	-4.3
2 Savings from integration of government departments and the reduction in benefit fraud		5.0	-5.0	-0.6
Health and education funding	**71.5**	**76.5**	**+5.0**	**+0.6**
Total net reduction in public expenditure			-35.0	-4.3
Reduction in Taxation				
Proposal				
1 Cost of raising initial personal income tax threshold			-55.0	-6.8
2 Reduction in income tax allowances			+20.0	+2.5
Total reduction in tax revenue			-35.0	-4.3

NB These changes are consistent with reducing the UK tax burden to 33% of GDP.

A call to arms

History shows that radical ideas tend to divide people.

On one side are arranged the forces of those who say that nothing can be done, joined by those who think that nothing needs to be done.

On the other side are aligned those people who believe something has to be done and that it can be done.

This pamphlet is dedicated to the latter group.

SCHEDULE OF BENEFITS

ATTENDANCE ALLOWANCE
higher rate
lower rate

CHILD BENEFIT
only, elder or eldest for whom child benefit is payable (couple)
only, elder or eldest for whom child benefit is payable (lone parent)
each subsequent child

CHILD'S SPECIAL ALLOWANCE
see note on Child Dependency Increase

COUNCIL TAX BENEFIT
Personal allowances
– single
– 18 to 24
– 25 or over
– lone parent – 18 or over
– couple – one or both over 18
Dependent Children
– birth to September following 11th birthday
– from September following 11th birthday to September following 16th birthday
– from September following 16th birthday to day before 19th birthday
Premiums
– family
– family (lone parent rate)
– pensioner
– single
– couple
Pensioner (enhanced)
– single
– couple
Pensioner (higher)
– single
– couple
Disability
Severe disability
– single
– couple (one qualifies)
– couple (both qualify)
Disabled child

Carer
Allowance for personal expenses for claimants in hospital
– higher rate
– lower rate
Non-dependant deductions
– aged 18 or over and in remunerative work
– gross income: £255 or more
– gross income: £204 - £254.99
– gross income: £118 - £203.99
– gross income less than £118
– others, aged 18 or over
Alternative maximum Council Tax Benefit
Second adult on Income Support or income based Jobseekers Allowance
Second adult's gross income :
– under £118
– £118 to £154.99
Capital
– upper limit
– amount disregarded
– child's limit
– upper limit for perm. res. Of RC/NH
– amt disregarded for perm. res. Of RC/NH
Tariff income
– £1 for every complete £250 or part thereof between amount of capital disregarded and capital upper limit
Earnings disregards
– where disability premium awarded
– various specified employments
– lone parent
– where the claimant has a partner
– single claimant
– where carer premium awarded
– childcare charges
– childcare charges (2 or more children)
– other income disregards
– maintenance disregard
– war disablement pension and war
– widow's pension
– certain voluntary and charitable payments
– student loan
– student's covenanted income
– income from boarders : disregard the fixed amount

(£20) plus 50% of the balance of the charge
- 30 Hr Adult Allowance in DWA
- 30 Hr Adult Credit in FC
Expenses for subtenants
- furnished or unfurnished
- where heating is included, additional

DEPENDENCY INCREASES
Adult Dependency Increases
For spouse or person looking after children, with retirement pension on own insurance, long term incap. Benefit, unemployability supplement
Severe disablement allowance
Invalid care allowance
Short-term incap. benefit if beneficiary over pension age
Maternity allowance/short-term incap. ben.
Child Dependency Increases, with retirement pension, widows benefit, short-term incap. ben at the higher rate long term incap. ben. Invalid care allowance severe disab. Allowance, higher rate industrial death benefit, unemployability supplement and short-term incap. benefit if beneficiary over pension age

DISABILITY LIVING ALLOWANCE
Care Component
- Highest
- Middle
- Lowest
Mobility Component
- Higher
- Lower

DISABILITY WORKING ALLOWANCE
Adult allowance
Single people
Couples/Lone Parents
30 Hours Allowance
Child allowance
- from birth
- from September following 11th birthday
- from September following 16th birthday
Applicable amount (ie taper threshold)
Single People
Couples/Lone Parents
Disabled Child's Allowance
Capital
- upper limit
- amount disregarded
- child's limit
Tariff income
- £1 for every complete £250 or part thereof between amount of capital disregarded and capital upper limit
Disregards
- maintenance disregard
- war disablement pension and war widow's pension
- certain voluntary and charitable payments
- student loan
- student's covenanted income
- income from boarders: disregard the fixed amount (£20) plus 50% of the balance of the charge

- childcare charges
- childcare charges (2 or more children)
- Expenses for subtenants
- furnished or unfurnished
- where heating is included, additional

EARNINGS RULES
Invalid Care Allowance
Limit of earnings from councillor's allowance
Therapeutic earnings limit
Industrial injuries unemployability
Supplement permitted earnings level (annual amount)
War pensioners' unemployability supplement permitted earnings level (annual amount)
Adult dependency increases with short-term incap. benefit where claimant is
      (a) under pension age
      (b) over pension age
Maternity allowance
Retirement pension, long-term incap. ben., severe disablement allowance, unemployability supplement where dependant
      (a) is living with claimant
      (b) still qualifies for the tapered earnings rule
severe disablement allowance where dependant not living with claimant
Invalid care allowance
Child dependency increases level at which CDIs are affected by earnings of claimant's spouse or partner
- for first child
- for each subsequent child

FAMILY CREDIT
Adult credit
30 hours credit
Child credits
- from birth
- from September following 11th birthday
- from September following 16th birthday
Applicable amount (ie: threshold)
Capital
- Upper limit
- Amount disregarded
- Child's limit
Assumed income from capital
£1 for every £250 or part of £250 between amount of capital disregarded and capital upper limit
Disregards
- maintenance disregard
- war disablement pension and war widow's pension
- certain voluntary and charitable payments
- student loan
- student's covenanted income
- income from boarders:
- disregard the fixed amount (£20) plus 50% of the balance of the charge
- childcare charges
- childcare charges (2 or more children)
Expenses for subtenants furnished or unfurnished where heating is included, additional

APPENDIX 1

GUARDIAN'S ALLOWANCE
See note on Child Dependency Increase

HOSPITAL DOWNRATING
20% rate
40% rate

HOUSING BENEFIT
Personal allowances
– single
– 16 to 24
– 25 or over
– lone parent
– under 18
– 18 or over
– couple
– both under 18
– one or both over 18
– dependent children
– birth to September following 11th birthday
– from September following 11th birthday to September following 16th birthday
– from September following 16th birthday to day before 19th birthday
Premiums
– family
– family (lone parent rate)
Pensioner
– single
– couple
Pensioner (enhanced)
– single
– couple
Pensioner (higher)
– single
– couple
Disability
– single
– couple
Severe disability
– single
– couple (one qualifies)
– couple (both qualify)
– disabled child
– carer
Allowance for personal expenses for claimants in hospital
– higher rate
– lower rate
Non-dependent deductions, rent rebates and allowances aged 25 and over, in receipt of Income Support or income based Job Seekers Allowance aged 18 or over, not in remunerative work or gross income less than £80.00
– aged 18 or over and in remunerative work
– gross income: less than £80.00
– gross income: £80 to £117.99
– gross income: £118 to £154.99
– gross income: £155 to £203.99
– gross income: £204.00 to £254.99
– gross income: £255.00 and above
Service charges for fuel
– heating
– hot water
– lighting
– cooking
Amount ineligible for meals
– three or more meals a day
– single claimant
– each person in family aged 16 or over
– each child under 16
– less than three meals a day
– single claimant
– each person in family aged 16 or over
– each child under 16
– breakfast only – claimant and each member of family
Capital
– upper limit
– amount disregarded
– child's limit
– upper limit for perm. res. of RC/NH
– amt disregarded for perm. res. of RC/NH
Tariff income
£1 for every complete £250 or part thereof between amount of capital disregarded and capital upper limit
Earnings disregards
– where disability premium awarded
– various specified employments
– lone parent
– where the claimant has a partner
– single claimant
– where carer premium awarded
– childcare charges
– childcare charges (2 or more children)
Other income disregards
– maintenance disregards
– war disablement pension and war
– widow's pension
– certain voluntary and charitable payments
– student loan
– student's covenanted income
– income from boarders:
– disregard the fixed amount (£20) plus
– 50% of the balance of the charge
– 30 Hr Adult Allowance in DWA
– 30 Hr Adult Credit in FC
Expenses for subtenants
– furnished or unfurnished
– where heating is included, additional

INCAPACITY BENEFIT
Long-term incapacity Benefit
Short-term incapacity Benefit
(under pension age)
– lower rate
– higher rate
Short-term incapacity Benefit
(over pension age)
– lower rate
– higher rate
Increase of Long-term Incap. Ben for age
– higher rate
– lower rate
Invalidity Allowance (Transitional)
– higher rate
– middle rate
– lower rate

THE WAR OF INDEPENDENCE – A DECLARATION

INCOME SUPPORT
Personal Allowances
- single
- under 18 – usual rate
- under 18 – higher rate payable
- in specific circumstances
- 18 to 24
- 25 or over

Lone parent
- under 18 – usual rate
- under 18 – higher rate payable
- in specific circumstances
- 18 or over

Couple
- both under 18
- one or both 18 or over
- Dependent children
- birth to September following 11th birthday
- from September following 11th birthday to September following 16th birthday
- from September following 16th birthday to day before 19th birthday

Residential Allowance except Greater London
- Greater London

Premiums
- family
- family (lone parent rate)

Pensioner
- single
- couple

Pensioner (enhanced)
- single
- couple

Pensioner (higher)
- single
- couple

Disability
- single
- couple
- severe disability
- single
- couple (one qualifies)
- couple (both qualify)

Disabled child
- carer

Maximum amounts for accommodation and meals in residential care homes
- old age
- very dependent elderly
- mental disorder (not handicap)

Allowances for personal expenses for claimants in:
- the Polish home Ilford Park
- max amount for accommodation and meals
- personal expenses for claimant
- personal expenses for partner
- personal expenses for dep children
    - (a) under 11
    - (b) 11 to 15
    - (c) 16 to 17
    - (d) 18

Housing costs
- deduction for non-dependants
- aged 25 and over, in receipt of Income Support
- or income based Job Seekers Allowance
-

- aged 18 or over, not in work or gross income less than £80.00

Aged 18 or over and in remunerative work:
- gross income: £80 to £117.99
- gross income: £118 to £154.99
- gross income: £155 to £203.99
- gross income: £204.00 to £254.99
- gross income: £255.00 and above

Deduction for direct payments
- arrears of housing, fuel and water costs
- council tax and fines default

Deductions for child maintenance (standard)
Deductions for child maintenance (lower)
Arrears of Community Charge
- court order against claimant
- ourt order against couple

Maximum rates for recovery of overpayments
- ordinary overpayments
- where claimant convicted of fraud
- drug/alcohol dependence
- mental handicap
- physical disablement
- (a) (under pension age)
- (b) (over pension age)
- others
- maximum Great London increase
- nursing homes
- mental disorder (not handicap)
- drug/alcohol dependence
- mental handicap
- terminal illness
- physical disablement
- (a) (under pension age)
- (b) (over pension age)
- others (including elderly)
- maximum Greater London increase

Amounts for meals where these cannot be purchased with the accommodation
- (Daily Rate)
- breakfast
- midday meal
- evening meal

Allowances for personal expenses for claimants in Private and voluntary residential care and nursing homes
- personal expenses
- dependent children
    - (a) under 11
    - (b) 11 to 15
    - (c) 16 to 17
    - (d) age 18

Hospital
- higher rate
- lower rate

Local authority (Pt III) accommodation
- of which, Personal Expenses

Reduction in benefit for strikers
Capital
- upper limit
- amount disregarded
- child's limit
- upper limit for perm. res. of RC/NH
- amt disregarded for perm. res. of RC/NH

Tariff income

APPENDIX 1

£1 for every complete £250 or part thereof between amount of capital disregarded and capital upper limit
Disregards
– standard earnings
– couples earnings
– higher earnings
– war disablement pension and war
– widow's pension
– voluntary and charitable payments
– student loan
– student's covenanted income
– income from boarders:
– disregard the fixed amount (£20) plus
– 50% of the balance of the charge
– Expenses for subtenants
– furnished or unfurnished
– where heating is included, additional

INDUSTRIAL DEATH BENEFIT
Widow's pension
– higher rate
– lower rate

INDUSTRIAL DISABLEMENT PENSION
18 and over, or under 18 with dependants
– 100%; 90%; 80%; 70%; 60%; 50%; 40%; 30%; 20%
Under 18
– 100%; 90%; 80%; 70%; 60%; 50%; 40%; 30%; 20%
Maximum life gratuity (lump sum)
Unemployability Supplement plus where appropriate an increase for early incapacity
– higher rate
– middle rate
– lower rate
Maximum reduced earnings allowance
Maximum retirement allowance
Constant attendance allowance
– exceptional rate
– intermediate rate
– normal maximum rate
– part-time rate
Exceptionally severe disablement allowance

JOBSEEKERS ALLOWANCE
Contribution based JSA – Pers. Rates
– under 18
– 18 to 24
– 25 or over
Income-based JSA – pers. Allowances
– under 18
– 18 to 24
– 25 or over
– lone parent
– under 18 – usual rate
– under 18 – higher rate payable
– in specific circumstances
– 18 or over
– couple
– both under 18
– both under 18, one disabled
– both under 18, with resp. for a child
– one under 18, one 18-24

– one under 18, one 25+
– both 18 or over
– dependent children
– birth to Sept. following 11th birthday
– from Sept. following 11th birthday to Sept. following 16th birthday
– from Sept. following 16th birthday to day before 19th birthday
Residential Allowance
– Except Greater London
– Greater London
Premiums
– family
– family (lone parent rate)
– pensioner
– single couple
– pensioner (enhanced)
– couple
– pensioner (higher)
– single
– couple
– disability
– single
– couple
– severe disability
– single
– couple (one qualifies)
– couple (both qualify)
– disabled child
– carer
Maximum amounts for accommodation and meals in
– residential care homes
– mental disorder (not handicap)
– drug/alcohol dependence
– mental handicap
– physical disablement
– (under pension age)
– others
– maximum Greater London increase
– nursing homes
– mental disorder (not handicap)
– drug/alcohol dependence
– mental handicap
– terminal illness
– physical disablement
– (under pension age)
– others (including elderly)
– maximum Greater London increase
Amounts for meals where these cannot be purchased within the accommodation
– (Daily Rate)
– breakfast
– midday meal
– evening meal
Allowances for personal expenses for claimants in private and voluntary residential care and nursing homes
– personal expenses
– dependent children
– under 11
– 11 to 15
– 16 to 17
– age 18
– hospital
– higher rate

THE WAR OF INDEPENDENCE – A DECLARATION

- lower rate
- local authority (Pt III) accommodation
- of which, Personal Expenses

Housing costs
- Deduction deduction for non-dependants
- aged 25 and over, in receipt of Income Support
  or income based Job Seekers allowance
- aged 18 or over, not in remunerative work or
- gross income less than £80.00
- gross income : £80 to £117.99
- gross income: £118 to £154.99
- gross income: £155 to £203.99
- gross income: £204.00 to £254.99
- gross income: £255.00 and above

for direct payments
Deductions from JSA (IB)
- arrears of housing, fuel and water costs
- council tax and fines default

Deductions for Child Maintenance
- deductions for child maintenance (standard)
- deductions for child maintenance (lower)

Arrears of Community Charge
- court order against claimant
- court order against couple

Deductions from JSA (Cont.)
Arrears of Comm. Charge, Council Tax and fines
- Age 16 – 17
- Age 18 – 24
- Age 25+

Max. dedn for arrears of Child Supp.Maintenance
- Age 16 – 17
- Age 18 – 24
- Age 25+

Maximum rates for recovery of overpayments
- ordinary overpayments
- where claimant convicted of fraud

Reduction in benefit for strikers
- Capital
- upper limit
- amount disregarded
- child's limit
- upper limit for perm. res. of RC/NH
- amt disregarded for perm. res. of RC/NH
- Tariff income
- £1 for every complete £250 or part
- thereof between amount of capital
- disregarded and capital upper limit

Disregards
- standard earnings
- couples earnings
- higher earnings
- war disablement pension and war widow's
  pension
- voluntary and charitable payments
- student loan
- student's covenanted income
- income from boarders:
- disregard the fixed amount (£20) plus
- 50% of the balance of the charge

Expenses for subtenants
- furnished or unfurnished
- where heating is included, additional

MATERNITY ALLOWANCE
Lower rate

Higher rate

PNEUMOCONIOSIS, BYSSINOSIS, WORKMEN'S COMPENSATION (SUPPLEMENTATION) AND OTHER SCHEMES
Total disablement allowance and major
Incapacity allowance (maximum)
Partial disablement allowance
Unemployability supplement
- plus where appropriate increases
- for early incapacity
- higher rate
- middle rate
- lower rate

Constant attendance allowance
- exceptional rate
- intermediate rate
- normal maximum rate
- part-time rate

Exceptionally severe disablement allowance
Lesser incapacity allowance
- maximum rate of allowance
- based on loss of earnings over

RETIREMENT PENSION
Category A or B
Category B (lower) – husband's insurance
Category C or D – non-contributory
Category C (lower) – non-contributory
Additional pension
Increments to:-
- Basic & additional pensions
- Contracted out deductions (CODs) (Pre Apr '88
  earnings)
- Graduate Retirement Benefit (GRB)
- Increments to CODs (Apr.88 – Apr. 96 earngs)
- (3.0% paid by schemes)

Graduate Retirement Benefit (unit) (pence)
Graduate Retirement Benefit (Inherited)
Additional at age 80

SEVERE DISABLEMENT ALLOWANCE
Basic rate
Age-related addition (from Dec 90)
Higher rate
Middle rate
Lower rate

STATUTORY MATERNITY PAY
Earnings threshold
Lower Rate

STATUTORY SICK PAY
Earnings threshold
Standard rate

WAR PENSIONS
Disablement Pension (100% rates)
- officer (£ per annum)
- other ranks

Age allowances
- 40%-50%
- over 50% but not over 70%
- over 70% but not over 90%
- over 90%

APPENDIX 1

Disablement gratuity
- specified minor injury (min.)
- specified minor injury (max.)
- unspecified minor injury (min.)
- unspecified minor injury (max.)

Unemployability allowance
- personal
- adult dependency increase
- increase for first child
- increase for subsequent children

Invalidity allowance
- higher rate
- middle rate
- lower rate

Constant attendance allowance
- exceptional rate
- intermediate rate
- normal maximum rate
- part-time rate

Comforts allowance
- higher rate
- lower rate

Mobility supplement

Allowance for lowered standard of occupation (maximum)

Exceptionally severe disablement allowance

Severe disablement occupational allowance

Clothing allowance (£ per annum, max.)

Education allowance (£ per annum max.)

War widow's pension

Widow (private)

Widow (NCO)

Widow – Officer (£ per annum max)

Childless widow u-40 (private)

Childless widow u-40 (NCO)

Childless widow u-40 (Officer £ per annum max)

Supplementary Pension

Age allowance
   (a) age 65 to 69
   (b) age 70 to 79
   (c) age 80 and over
- children's allowance
- increase for fist child
- (adjusted for ChB increase)
- increase for subsequent children

Orphan's pension
- increase for first child
- (adjusted for ChB increase)
- increase for subsequent children

Unmarried dependant living as spouse (max)

Rent allowance (maximum)

Adult orphan's pension (maximum)

Widower's pension

Private (max)

Officer (£ per annum max)

WIDOW'S BENEFIT

Widow's payment (lump sum)

Widowed mother's allowance

Widow's pension
- standard rate
- age-related
- age 54 (49); 53 (48); 52 (47); 51 (46); 50 (45); 49 (44); 48 (43); 47 (42); 46 (41); 45 (40)

Note: For deaths occurring before 11 April 1988

- Refer to age-points shown in brackets.

Scheme A

Credit
- couple
- single 25 and over
- single under 25
- for working 30 hrs+ pw

Applicable amount (ie taper threshold)
- couple
- single 25 and over
- single under 25

Scheme B

Credit
- couple
- single 25 and over
- single under 25
- for working 30 hrs+ pw

Applicable amount (ie taper threshold)
- couple
- single 25 and over
- single under 25

Both Schemes
- Capital upper limit
- amount disregarded

Tariff income
- £1 for every complete £250 or part
- thereof between amount of capital
- disregarded and capital upper limit
-

Source: DSS Internet site, April 1999

APPENDIX 2

SCHEDULE OF TAX ALLOWANCES, RELIEFS AND EXEMPTIONS

TAX ALLOWANCES:
Occupational pension schemes
Contributions to personal pensions (including retirement annuity premia and FSAVCs)
Life assurance premiums (for contracts made prior to 14 March 1984)
Private medical insurance premiums for the over 60s
Mortgage interest
Approved profit sharing schemes
Approved discretionary share option schemes
Approved savings-related share option schemes
Venture Capital Trusts
Enterprise Investment Scheme
Profit related pay
First £30,000 of payments on termination of employment
Interest on National Savings Certificates including index-linked Certificates
Premium Bond prizes
SAYE
Income of charities
Foreign service allowance paid to Crown servants abroad
First £8,000 of reimbursed relocation packages provided by employers
Gains arising on disposal of only or main residence
Retirement relief
Re-investment relief
Agricultural property relief
Business property relief
Heritage property and maintenance funds
Transfers to charities on death
Double taxation relief
Reduced rate of corporation tax on policy holders' fraction of profits
Contracted-out rebate occupational schemes of which:
−   Occupational schemes deducted from National Insurance Contributions received
−   Occupational schemes (COMPS) paid by Contributions Agency direct to scheme
−   Personal pensions
Married couple's allowance
Age-related allowances
Additional personal allowance for one parent family
Relief for maintenance payments
Child special allowance
Guardian's allowance
NI child dependency additions
Severe disablement allowance
Allowances to rehabilitees

Maternity allowance
£10 Christmas bonus for pensioners
Pensions and annuities paid to holders of the Victoria Cross and certain other gallantry awards
Children's allowance to Forces' widows
Disability working allowance
Widows' payments
Benefit of medical expenses paid by employer when employee falls sick when abroad
Benefit of alterations to accommodation by reason of employment
Special security measures
Certain expenses of MPs
Benefit of workplace sports facilities
Outplacement counselling for redundant employees
Accelerated capital allowances for Enterprise Zones

TAX EXEMPTIONS:
British government securities where owner not ordinarily resident in the United Kingdom
Child benefit (including one parent benefit)
Long-term incapacity benefit
Industrial disablement benefits
Attendance allowance
Disability living allowance
War disablement benefits
War widows pension
Small companies' reduced rate of corporation tax
Indexation allowance and rebasing to march 1982
Taper relief
Annual exempt amount (half of the individuals' exemption for trustees)
Gains accrued but unrealised at death
Nil rate inheritance tax band for chargeable transfers not exceeding the threshold
Inheritance tax on transfers on death to surviving spouses
Stamp duty of transfers of land and property where the consideration does not exceed the threshold
Reduced National Insurance contributions for self-employed not attributable to reduce benefit eligibility
Widow's bereavement allowance
Blind person's allowance
First £70 of National Savings Bank ordinary account interest
Short-term lower rate incapacity benefit
Certain personal incidental expenses
Charitable donations under the payroll giving scheme

THE WAR OF INDEPENDENCE – A DECLARATION

Student maintenance awards
Trade unions: investment income applied to provident benefits
Agricultural societies on profits of shows
Officials and agents of overseas governments etc.
Visiting forces, other than UK citizens
Inter-governmental organisations
Unremitted income of taxpayers resident but not domiciled in the UK
Certain statutory and public bodies and local authorities
Funds held for reducing the National Debt
Income of Trustee Savings Banks from investments with the National Debt Commissioners
Discount element of certain gilts issued at a discount
Accrued income of small investors whose nominal value of holding of securities does not exceed £5,000
Subsidised canteen meals provided for an employer's staff generally
Benefit of living accommodation and associated costs provided to certain groups of employees
Beneficial loans below £5,000
Benefit of entertainment provided for employees by third parties
Car parking at or near an employee's place of work
Retraining expenditure
Friendly societies
Futures and options – examples for authorised unit trusts and pension schemes
Workplace nurseries
Unit trusts from full rate of corporation tax (reduced rate applies)
Company car accessories for the disabled
Unremitted gains of taxpayers resident but not domiciled in the UK
Gains of charities and scientific research organisations
Gains of approved pension schemes
Gains of unit trusts for exempt unit-holders
Gains accruing to authorised unit trusts and approved investment trusts
Actual and deemed gains of settlements on death of life tenant
Gains arising on disposal of:
– Motor cars
– Chattels which are wasting assets
– Other chattels if value is £6,000 or less on disposal
– Assets by way of gifts to the nation
– Savings certificates and securities issued under the National Loans Act 1968
– Decorations for valour
– Contracts for deferred annuities
– Interests under a settlement
– Currency for personal expenditure outside the UK
– Life assurance policies
Gains arising from:
– Betting winnings
– Compensation or damages for wrong or injury
– Grants of purchased annuities
– Compensation or damages for wrong or injury
– Grants of purchased annuities
Lifetime transfers between spouses

Gifts of £3,000 each year
Gifts of £250 per donee
Normal gifts out of income
Gifts in consideration of marriage
Lifetime transfers to charities
Gifts to political parties
Foreign pensions and foreign armed forces pay
Cash options under approved annuity schemes
Certain savings by persons domiciled in the Channel Islands or the Isle of Man
Foreign currency bank accounts
Waivers of dividends and remuneration
Reversionary interests
Transfers to employee trusts
Settled property passing to settlor, spouse or widow
Accumulation and maintenance settlements
Trusts for mentally or physically disabled
Death on active service
Trade or professional compensation funds
Charitable trusts
Employee and newspaper trusts
Protective trusts
Superannuation schemes
Distributions out of discretionary trusts to charities, political parties etc.
Estate duty surviving spouse settlements
Transfers of land to registered housing associations
Transfers of stock on sale to market makers or recognised intermediaries
Transfers between associated companies
Transfers of building society shares
Issues or transfers of bearer instruments in foreign currencies
Transfers of Commonwealth government stocks and certain loan stocks
Transfers to a Minister of the Crown
Transfers to charities
Other minor stamp duty exemptions
Transfers under stock borrowing and sale and repurchase arrangements
Limitation of duty payable on purchases of public sector dwellings
Limitation of duty payable on borrowings of stock by market makers
Purchases by issuing houses in connection with public issues
Purchases by market makers or recognised intermediaries
Purchases under stock borrowing and sale and repurchase arrangements
Purchases of securities by broker/dealers where the securities are resold within 7 days
Purchases by managers of units under a unit trust scheme
Purchases by charities
Purchases of certain bearer instruments

TAX RELIEF FOR:
Instalment relief on share options exercised outside approved schemes
Expenditure on property managed as one estate
Farming etc averaging of profits
Post-trading expenditure
Rent-a-room
Special security measures

APPENDIX 2

Professional subscriptions
Vocational training
Relief to investment companies for losses on unquoted shares in trading companies
Relief for trading losses against capital gains
Quick succession relief
Taper relief on transfers between three to seven years before death
Double taxation relief
Woodlands relief

ROLLOVER/HOLDOVER RELIEF FOR:

Gifts of assets
Transfers of businesses to companies
Transfers of non-United Kingdom trades to non-resident companies
Sales of shares to employee share ownership trusts
Replacement of business assets
Compensation used to restore damaged assets
Small part-disposals of land
Small capital distributions in respect of shares
Reorganisations of share capital
Reconstructions and amalgamations of companies
Gains on disposals
– within a group of companies
– of shares in return for gilts on compulsory acquisition
– assets between spouses
– other qualifying reliefs
Exit charge on company migration

ALLOWANCES AND RELIEFS FOR:

Pre-trading expenditure
Demergers
Industrial and Provident societies
Co-operative associations
Housing associations
Company's purchase of its own shares
Qualifying interest on loans not for the purchase of owner-occupied etc. property
Schedule E work expenses
Foreign earnings of employees working abroad for 365 days or more: 100 per cent deduction
Certain income of non-residents received through UK representatives
Foreign pensions
Lloyds underwriters: special reserve fund arrangement
Interest paid by companies on quoted Eurobonds
Income tax relief for losses on unquoted shares in trading companies
Certain foreign travel expenses
Transfers of securities under approved stock lending arrangements
Payments to trustees for approved profit sharing schemes
Payments to relevant scientific research associations
Payments for technical education relevant to a taxpayer's trade
Business contributions to Training and Enterprise Councils and Local Enterprise Councils
Employee priority allocations in public share offers

Payments to ESOP Trusts
Employer provided work related training
Payments from sickness and unemployment insurance policies
Indexation allowance & rebasing to March 1982 for companies
Double taxation of capital gains realised by individuals or trustees
Losses on disposals of assets between spouses
Chattels exceeding £6,000 in value (marginal relief)
Disposals by political party associations following boundary changes
Loans to traders
Gains on stock lending
Irrecoverable bonds
Land acquired by authorities with compulsory purchase powers
Falls in value of property before death or after death
Interest-free instalments
Double charges
Lloyd's premiums trust funds
Gifts for the maintenance of the family
Gifts for national purposes or for public benefit
Government securities owned by non-United Kingdom domiciled persons

Source: The Financial Statement and Budget Report (HC 298, 1998-99)

APPENDIX 3

BUDGET 99 MEASURES TO ALTER ALLOWANCES, RELIEFS, EXEMPTIONS

Corporation tax: new 10 per cent rate for the smallest companies from April 2000
Extension of first year capital allowances for SMEs at 40 per cent, for one year
Research and development tax credit
Tax relief for employer-loaned computers
Individual Learning Accounts: making employer contributions to employee ILAs tax and NICs free
Abolition of Vocational Training Relief (VTR)

INCOME TAX:
Indexation of most allowances and limits
New 10 per cent rate from April 1999
Basic rate reduced to 22 per cent from April 2000

NATIONAL INSURANCE CONTRIBUTIONS:
Indexation of thresholds
Alignment of threshold with income tax personal allowance, in two stages, beginning April 2000
Increases to upper earnings limits for employee contributions in April 2000 and April 2001
Reform of self-employment contribution rates and profits limits from April 2000
Reduction in employer contribution rate by 0.5 percentage points from April 2001

BENEFITS:
New Deal package for the over 50s: Employment Credit
Income Support: two week extension for lone parents moving into work
Abolition of married couples allowance from April 2000 for those born after 5 April 1935
Introduction of Children's Tax Credit from April 2001:
- with increases in Income Support child premia
- and with increases in Working Families Tax Credit and Disabled Person's Tax Credit

Child Benefit: indexation of rates and uprating from April 2000 to £15 per week for first child and £10 per week for subsequent children
Sure Start Maternity Grant
Maternity pay reforms
Increasing personal allowances for older people
Increase minimum income guarantee for pensioners
£100 Winter Allowance from 1999
Abolition of mortgage interest relief from April 2000
Countering avoidance in the provision of personal services
Extension of employer national insurance contributions to all benefits in kind which are subject to income tax from April 2000
Controlled Foreign Companies (CFCs): taxation of dividends
Capital gains on sale of companies
Stamp duty: compliance
VAT: changes to partial exemption rules
VAT: group treatment
Enlarging of VAT exemption on financing arrangements
VAT: bringing supplies by certain organisations in line with trade unions and professional bodies
Taxation of reverse premiums
Climate change levy
Energy efficiency measures and support for renewable energy sources
Green transport plans

APPENDIX 3

Increase in minor oils duties
Hydrocarbon oil duty escalator
Cut in duty on higher octane unleaded petrol
Company car taxation: reduction in business mileage discounts from April
Landfill tax: introduction of five year escalator

VEHICLE EXCISE DUTY:
Graduated VED – reduction of charge for small cars and indexation for others
New VED for heavy lorries
Freeze other lorry VED

Tobacco – aligning escalator with Budget day, freeze handrolled tobacco
Alcohol – aligning revalorisation point with Budget day and freeze
Gifts of equipment by businesses to charities
Inheritance tax: index threshold
Capital gains tax: rate adjustment
Vat: indexation of registration and deregistration thresholds
Football clubs: assistance for transition to new accounting rules
Revised rate of pools betting duty from 26.5 percent to 17.5 per cent
Removing the income tax charge on mobile phones
Stamp duty: 2.5 per cent rate for transfer of land and property above £250,000
and 3.5 per cent above £500,000
Increase in the rate of insurance premium tax by 1 percentage point (to 5 per cent)
VAT: option to tax land and property rules
Lloyd's insurance market: simplifying capital gains

Source: The Financial Statement and Budget Report (HC 298, 1998-99)

APPENDIX 4

CALCULATION OF INDEPENDENCE DAY 1999

Date	Working day number	Tax burden %	
Apr-01	64	25.3	
Apr-02	BH	25.3	
Apr-03	W	25.3	
Apr-04	W	25.3	
Apr-05	BH	25.3	
Apr-06	65	25.7	
Apr-07	66	26.1	
Apr-08	67	26.5	
Apr-09	68	26.9	
Apr-10	W	26.9	
Apr-11	W	26.9	
Apr-12	69	27.3	
Apr-13	70	27.7	
Apr-14	71	28.1	
Apr-15	72	28.5	
Apr-16	73	28.9	
Apr-17	W	28.9	
Apr-18	W	28.9	
Apr-19	74	29.2	
Apr-20	75	29.6	
Apr-21	**76**	**30.0**	**Target Independence Day**
Apr-22	77	30.4	
Apr-23	78	30.8	
Apr-24	W	30.8	
Apr-25	W	30.8	
Apr-26	79	31.2	
Apr-27	80	31.6	
Apr-28	81	32.0	
Apr-29	82	32.4	
Apr-30	83	32.8	
May-01	W	32.8	
May-02	W	32.8	
May-03	84	33.2	
May-04	85	33.6	
May-05	86	34.0	
May-06	87	34.4	
May-07	88	34.8	
May-08	W	34.8	
May-09	W	34.8	
May-10	89	35.2	
May-11	90	35.6	
May-12	91	36.0	
May-13	92	36.4	
May-14	93	36.8	
May-15	W	36.8	
May-16	W	36.8	
May-17	94	37.2	
May-18	**95**	**37.5**	**Independence Day based on 1998-99 tax ratio**
May-19	96	37.9	
May-20	97	38.3	
May-21	98	38.7	
May-22	W	38.7	
May-23	W	38.7	
May-24	99	39.1	
May-25	100	39.5	
May-26	101	39.9	
May-27	102	40.3	
May-28	103	40.7	
May-29	W	40.7	
May-30	W	40.7	
May-31	BH	40.7	

Total number of working weekdays = 260 minus 8 Bank Holidays plus 1 holiday reserved for Independence Day = 253

W : Weekend   **BH : Bank Holiday**
Example: Net taxes and compulsory social security contributions as % of GDP = 37.2% for 1998-99
                    Independence Day = Day (37.2% of 253) = Day 94.1 translates into Day 95 (May 18)

APPENDIX 5

BIBLIOGRAPHY

Bhattacharyya, Dilip K, *The Hidden Economy Estimates and Their Implications for Government Expenditure*, Deloitte & Touche Informal Economy Research Centre Working Paper No. 1, November 1998

Chennels, Lucy and Dilnot, Andrew (eds.) *The IFS Green Budget* (London: Institute for Fiscal Studies, January 1999)

Congdon, Tim "EMU and Tax Harmonization: How Much Will We Have to Pay?", Politeia lecture. 26 January 1999

DSS, *Households Below Average Income: A Statistical Analysis 1979-1994/95*, (London: The Stationery Office, 1997)

DSS, *The Abstract of Statistics for Social Security Benefits and Contributions*, 1995 Edition

DSS, *National Housing Benefit Accuracy Review 1997-98*

Employment Policy Institute, *Employment Audit*, Issue Nine, Autumn 1998

European Union *Business Investment Report*, 1998

Gosling A., Johnson P., McCrae J. and Paull G., *The Dynamics of Low Pay and Unemployment in early-1990s Britain*, Institute for Fiscal Studies, 1997

Gwartney, James and Lawson, Robert, *Economic Freedom of the World 1998-99 Interim Report* (Vancouver, B.C.: Fraser Institute, 1998)

HM Treasury, *Tax Ready Reckoner and Reliefs*, December 1997

HM Treasury, *Financial Statement and Budget Report*, March 1998

HM Treasury, *The Modernisation of Britain's Tax and Benefit System - Number Two; Work incentives: A Report by Martin Taylor*, March 1998

HM Treasury Green Paper, *Beating Fraud is Everyone's Business – Securing the Future*, July 1998

APPENDIX 5

HM Treasury, *Modern Public Services for Britain: Investing in Reform (Comprehensive Spending Review: new public spending plans 1999-2002)*, Cm 4011, July 1998

HM Treasury, *Pre-Budget Report*, Cm 4076, November 1998

HM Treasury, *Economic and Fiscal Strategy Report and Financial Statement and Budget Report*, HC 298, March 1999

Inland Revenue Statistics (London: The Stationery Office, 1998)

Inland Revenue, *Bicentenary of Income Tax 1799-1999: A brief history of Income Tax*, December 1998

International Monetary Fund, *International Financial Statistics Yearbook*, (Washington D.C.: IMF, 1998)

Kay, John and King, Mervyn *The British Tax System*, (Oxford: Oxford University Press, 5th edn. 1990)

Lewis, Russell, *The Deadweight State*, Economic Research Council research Study no. 15, 1998

McCrae, Julian "Simplifying the Formal Structure of UK Income Tax", *Fiscal Studies*, vol. 18, no. 3, (Aberdeen: BPC-AUP Aberdeen, 1997)

Market Opinion Research International *British Public Opinion* (various issues)

Matthews, Kent and Lloyd-Williams, Jean, *VAT Evasion in Selected Sectors of the Economy: A Preliminary Examination*, Cardiff Business School, University of Wales, Cardiff, 1998

Matthews, Kent, *VAT Harmonisation in the EU: Is there a European Laffer Curve for VAT?*, Cardiff Business School, University of Wales, Cardiff, June 1998

OECD Economic Outlook, "Fiscal Consolidation and the Effectiveness of the Public Sector" (Paris: OECD, June 1997)

OECD Economic Outlook, (Paris: OECD, June 1998)

OECD Revenue Statistics 1965-1996 (Paris: OECD, 1997)

Office for National Statistics, *Public Finance Trends 96* (London: HMSO, 1996)

Office for National Statistics, *Financial Statistics*, October 1998

Parker, Hermione, *Taxes, Benefits and Family Life*, IEA Research Monograph 50 , 1995

SOME RECENT CPS PUBLICATIONS

CONSERVATIVISM, DEMOCRACY & NATIONAL IDENTITY £5.00
John O'Sullivan

Languishing in Britain and, indeed, across Europe, the right seems to be unsure of its relevance to current political debate. But Conservatism comes into its own when there is a sense that existing institutions and beliefs are under threat. There is a latent threat which may give rise to a revival of the conservative spirit: the gradual and insidious undermining of democracy by numerous agencies – the EU, the courts, bureaucrats – and by various ideologies – most particularly multiculturalism. These areas will be the new battleground for the right. The fight to defend democracy is now the crucial battle for all conservatives.

...a brilliant lecture – Michael Gove, *The Times*

MORAL EVASION £7.50
David Selbourne

Too many participants in ethical debates misrepresent the issues before us, or avoid responsibility for their own conduct, or discredit by use of falsehood those whose arguments they disapprove. At one extreme, it is said that nothing can any longer be done about our moral condition. Or, at another extreme, that nothing needs to be done about it, since there is nothing fundamentally at fault in our moral condition in the first place. But questions about 'the moral order' deserve to stand at the centre of public and political controversy in the coming period. They must not, as they all too often are, be evaded.

...an excellent pamphlet – Stephen Glover, *The Spectator*

SERIOUS DAMAGE –THE WITHHOLDING TAX & THE CITY OF LONDON £5.00
Richard Baron

The proposed European "Withholding Tax" could drive the London bond market offshore by imposing heavy financial and administrative costs. In addition, the Government's failure to veto the tax has sent a clear message to City institutions: their interests are negotiable. The bond market is highly mobile. Ten financial institutions, all foreign owned, issued two thirds of bonds issued in London in 1998. These institutions can – and will – move their London operations if they feel that their interests are better understood elsewhere. And the Withholding Tax is being threatened at the very time that Switzerland is doing all it can to attract a larger slice of the global bond trading market. The Government must veto this tax now if it is to prevent serious damage to the City.

TIME BOMB UNDER THE CITY – Headline in the *Evening Standard*

A Subscription to the Centre for Policy Studies

The Centre for Policy Studies runs an Associate Membership Scheme which is available at £55.00 per year (or £50.00 if paid by bankers' order). Associates are entitled to all CPS Policy Studies produced in a 12-month period (of which there at least ten); previous publications at *half* their published price; and (whenever possible) reduced fees for the conferences which the Centre holds.

For more details please write or telephone to:
The Secretary
Centre for Policy Studies
57 Tufton Street, London SW1P 3QL
Tel: 0171 222 4488   Fax: 0171 222 4388   website: cps.org.uk